CULINARY TREASURES

DUDE & GUEST RANCHES *of* AMERICA

SHERRY MONAHAN

OTTERFORD GOURMET
BENTONVILLE, ARKANSAS • HEBER CITY, UTAH

OTTERFORD GOURMET

An Imprint of Roan & Weatherford Publishing Associates, LLC
Bentonville, Arkansas • Heber City, Utah
www.roanweatherford.com

Copyright © 2025 by Sherry Monahan

We are a strong supporter of copyright. Copyright represents creativity, diversity, and free speech, and provides the very foundation from which culture is built. We appreciate you buying the authorized edition of this book and for complying with applicable copyright laws by not reproducing, scanning, or distributing any part of it in any form without permission. Thank you for supporting our writers and allowing us to continue publishing their books.

This work is the product of human creativity and effort, crafted without the use of generative artificial intelligence in its writing or storytelling. While AI is a valuable tool in many creative fields, we are committed to publishing works by humans about the human experience. Without any limitations on the author or Roan & Weatherford Publishing Associates' exclusive copyright, any use of this publication to train generative artificial intelligence is expressly prohibited.

Library of Congress Cataloging-in-Publication Data
Names: Monahan, Sherry, author.
Title: Dude & Guest Ranches of America | Culinary Treasures #1
Description: First Edition | Bentonville: Otterford, 2025.
Identifiers: ISBN: 978-1-63373-041-7 (hardcover) |
ISBN: 978-1-63373-042-4 (trade paperback) | ISBN: 978-1-63373-043-1 (eBook)
Subjects: | BISAC: Cooking/Regional & Ethnic/American/Western States

Otterford Gourmet paperback edition November, 2025

Cover Design by Casey W. Cowan
Interior Design by Casey W. Cowan & George "Clay" Mitchell
Editing by Amy Cowan

This cookbook is a work of historical narrative and culinary exploration. While every effort has been made to accurately portray historical events, customs, and recipes, the author has occasionally drawn on creative interpretation and anecdotal sources to provide context and enrich the storytelling. Some details, including names and locations, may have been modified or adapted for narrative clarity. The recipes included are inspired by historical practices but have been adjusted in some cases to suit modern kitchens and tastes. Readers should exercise caution when preparing recipes, especially those involving unfamiliar techniques or ingredients, and adapt them as necessary to meet dietary or safety considerations. This work is not intended to defame or misrepresent any individual, group, or entity. Any resemblance to actual persons, living or deceased, is purely coincidental.

To all the brave souls who called the West home.

---

*To all the foodies—past, present, and future.
Just remember, tomorrow may be the future,
but it soon becomes the past.*

---

*Lastly, to all my friends, fans, and family
for always asking and listening about my latest ideas!*

TABLE OF CONTENTS

- ★ INGREDIENT GUIDE — v
- ★ INTRODUCTION — vii
- ★ CAST IRON COOKING NOTES — ix
- ★ BREAKFAST & BREADS — 3
- ★ APPETIZERS, SOUP & SALADS — 19
- ★ SIDES, VEGETABLES, SEASONINGS & SAUCES — 33
- ★ MAIN DISHES & ENTREES — 45
- ★ DESSERTS & SNACKS — 71
- ★ INDEX — 95
- ★ RANCH GLOSSARY — 99
- ★ ACKNOWLEDGEMENTS — 107
- ★ ABOUT THE AUTHOR — 109

INGREDIENT GUIDE

For clarity in recipes, this code of ingredients will help ensure the dishes will turn out as intended. For recipes that call for Mason or canning jars, please sterilize the jars and lids according to the manufacturer's directions.

Ingredient Listed	Meaning
Flour	All-Purpose
Butter	Salted Butter
Milk	Whole Milk
Sugar	White, Granulated
Peppers	Green Bell
Onions	White
Eggs	Large
Spices	Ground

INTRODUCTION

What is it that intrigues us about dude and guest ranches? Possibly that people from all walks of life and all ages get to enjoy playing cowboy or cowgirl at them. Maybe it's the allure and enchantment of the Wild West with its wide-open spaces or lush green mountains. Maybe it's all the fun activities like roping, riding, and fishing that make guests feel like a good old ranch hand. Or maybe it's both.

The American West is something unique to this country, and nowhere else on Earth can its history be experienced but there. Regardless of why people enjoy spending time at these ranches, they all enjoy one common activity—eating. Some enjoy sitting around a campfire or eating at a chuckwagon event or being communal while eating in the dining room.

Dude and guest ranches were born out of the old west's necessity of ranches to house cowboys who tended livestock. Today's ranches, many of them dating back to the frontier cowboy days, allow guests to experience the cowboy way of life. Over the years, ranches have been creating recipes and serving meals to feed their cowboys and family members. As ranches sought to expand their income or even just survive, they began offering ranch experiences to the public.

Of course, guests need to eat, but dining at the ranch is more of an experience than a basic human need. That's why the menu offerings started to evolve. Some ranches offer classic staples that have been served since they first began operating, while others have embraced creativity and follow current trends. Many are historic or have historic ties with recipes passed down through generations.

Either way, ranch guests can expect to eat well. This book captures the stories of ranches and some of their classic recipes easily made in anyone's kitchen. There's nothing like being on a ranch out West, but being able to make one of their favorite recipes is the next best thing. And for those adventurous cooks, there's an outdoor Dutch oven cooking section on the next page.

Enjoy the cooking ride!

Sherry

CAST IRON COOKING NOTES

The first thing you need for cooking with cast iron is a well-seasoned cast-iron Dutch oven or frying pan. Please note that cooking with a Dutch oven takes practice, and while the following are basic guidelines, they may need to be adjusted depending upon the altitude, temperature, and wind. Because wind causes the briquettes to burn faster, try to dig a hole to protect the coals while cooking.

Remember that outdoor temperatures impact cooking times, so things will cook quicker when it's hot outside and slower when it's colder. Arrange the coals in a circle under the oven and evenly cover the top or place the briquettes in a checkerboard pattern for even heat distribution. Most coals should last between 30 to 45 minutes, so additional coals might be needed if cooking time is longer. Be sure to have additional coals ready to go on or under the oven as needed. When adding additional coals remember that, on average, each briquette produces about 10°–15°F worth of heat on a moderately warm day with no wind.

The number of coals used is based on the size of the Dutch oven. The temperature required to cook also matters, so baking something at 350°F in a 12-inch Dutch oven would require twenty-four briquettes in total. Eighteen briquettes would be placed on the top and six underneath. The basic formula when baking a recipe is to use twice the number of briquettes as the diameter of the Dutch oven with 3/4 of them on the lid. When frying or boiling, place all the coals underneath. For simmering, place 3/4 of them under the oven and 1/4 on the top.

Here's a handy chart for baking outside:

Oven Temp.	8"	8"	10"	10"	12"	12"	14"	14"	16"	16"
	Over	Under	Over	Under	Over	Under	Over	Under	Over	Under
300° F	9	3	12	4	15	5	18	6	21	7
325° F	10	3	14	4	17	5	20	6	23	7
350° F	11	5	13	7	16	8	21	7	24	8
375° F	14	4	17	5	20	6	23	7	26	8
400° F	15	5	18	6	21	7	24	8	27	9
425° F	17	5	20	6	23	7	26	8	29	9
450° F	18	6	21	7	24	8	27	9	30	10

DUDE & GUEST RANCHES
of AMERICA

CHAPTER ONE

BREAKFAST & BREADS

★ BREAKFAST RIDE POTATOES

White Stallion Ranch, Tucson, Arizona

The True family has been operating this ranch since 1965, but the property's history is much older than that. White Stallion Ranch was originally built in the 1900s and started as a cattle ranch constructed of Mexican adobe, which is brick made of mud and straw. During the renovation, wire and horseshoes were found in the walls.

It was homesteaded by David Young from 1936 to 1939, and he was the first deeded owner of the property. After that, Herbert and Vine Bruning purchased the property and used it as a ranch where they raised ranch cattle, chickens, and turkeys. They changed the name to CB Bar Ranch, and it was once home to 30,000 birds. In 1945, Max Zimmerman, a Chicago liquor store owner, bought the ranch and moved West. Max named the ranch the MZ Bar Ranch and turned it into a guest ranch. He constructed six buildings complete with kitchenettes for guests, and those buildings are still standing, but several renovations later they no longer resemble the original guest room interiors. In 1949, Mary Varner bought it and continued to operate it as a guest ranch, also offering long-term rentals to the nearby Marana Army Airfield. Then years later, Brew and Marge Towne of Cape Cod, Massachusetts, fulfilled their dream of owning a guest ranch and named it the White Stallion. They really wanted to name it the Black Stallion but reconsidered when they realized that the "BS Ranch" wasn't such a great idea.

It was 1965 when Allen and Cynthia True came from Colorado to make the ranch their home. Along with them were their sons Russell, who was just five years old, and Michael, who was still in a crib. At the time, the ranch consisted of seventeen rooms, seventeen horses, and two hundred acres. The number of guest ranches left in the area had dropped to about thirty, so Allen and Cynthia began purchasing adjacent land as it became available, which increased the ranch to 3,000 acres. The ranch serves up three squares a day, but those heading out for an early morning ride are treated to these potatoes. They're cooked the same way they have been for fifty plus years, which is out in the desert in the same cast iron pans over an open fire for guests on the breakfast ride. According to the ranch, "We use old baked potatoes and use up potatoes from dinners."

Serves 8-12

8 cups boiled potatoes	1. Cut the potatoes into pieces, about the size of a thumb.
2 1/2 tablespoons onion salt	2. Combine the seasonings together and toss with the potatoes.
1 3/4 teaspoons black pepper	
2/3 cup paprika	3. Add the bacon and mix together.
1 cup cooked, crumbled bacon	4. Heat the olive oil in a large pan over medium high heat.
2–4 tablespoons olive oil	5. Fry the potatoes until hot and then place in a large bowl.
	6. Serve when ready.

★ RED ROCK RANCH GREEN CHILI GRITS
Red Rock Ranch, Kelly, Wyoming

Around the time Wyoming gained statehood in 1890, a hearty group of trailblazers with nerves of steel ventured up to Gros Ventre valley in an effort to build a better life for themselves. The harsh realities of life back in the 1800s drew many out of the bustling cities but also made homesteading in the valley a survival of the fittest. The original four settlers of the Red Rock Ranch property laid claim around 1894. Not much is known about three of the settlers, but the fourth man was James Simpson. He was the last of the homesteaders who went on to open a drugstore in Jackson after selling his 160-acre parcel to William Redmond. William "'Bill"' Redmond married the sister of one of the original homesteaders and eventually became full owner of Red Rock Ranch. One of the first major changes of this time was the addition of the Redmond House in 1920.

Eugene and Agnes Meyer were the second owners of Red Rock Ranch. A Yale graduate turned financier and then newspaper publisher, Eugene was an influential leader in American social life. He published the Washington Post from 1933–1946, and the newspaper remained in the family for the rest of the 20th century. However, the finance and publishing world weren't his only passions. As the legend goes, he always wanted a ranch and a red Irish setter. Then, one night, he went to a dinner party and ended up with a ranch and a red Irish setter! Yearly summer visits from Washington D.C. to the ranch were coveted by the Meyer family, who cherished the peaceful trails and streams compared to the hustle and bustle of the East. Nonetheless, in 1943 as World War II intensified, a bittersweet decision had to be made. Red Rock Ranch was sold to an established local rancher who Meyer trusted to care for the land and its wildlife.

Red Rock Ranch's third owner was a pioneer aviator who also loved horses and the West. Major C.C. Moseley was born on July 21, 1894, in Boise, Idaho. He was a champion athlete and a fearless pilot during World War I. When he arrived in the Jackson Hole Valley in the early 1940s, he immediately set out to make a name for himself in ranching circles. He owned seven ranches in the area at various times. Blessed with a sharp eye, he was well known in the equestrian world as a top-notch horse breeder and commercial cattle dealer. Many changes were made to the land, like the addition of a main house and rudimentary communication between Jackson and the ranch. There was no power or telephone even in the 60s. It wasn't until 1969 that a system was installed to transmit messages to the ranch through the Sheriff's office. By the early 1970s, the ranch fell into a state of disrepair as Moseley's health began to fail. Like the other owners, Moseley was connected to the land and saw it as a sanctuary. When the sale of the ranch was imminent, he made it clear that it was not to be sold for redevelopment.

David and Deborah MacKenzie shared a similar vision for Red Rock Ranch and preserving its heritage. The new stewards, although from Illinois, were no strangers to the lure of the Wild West and had visited many times separately and together. As the legend goes, the MacKenzie's had attempted to visit Red Rock Ranch in the early 70s but turned around after reaching the iconic sign that remained for over fifty years: *End of Road–Red Rock Ranch–Not Open to Public.*

Years later, when the spirit of the West led the couple and young family to find a summer home, they landed back in the greater Teton area. The pull of Red Rock Ranch and its possibilities as

also a guest ranch and not only as a summer retreat sold the deal for the MacKenzies. By this time, a manager's house, guest house, and a little shop had been added to the property. However, they were dilapidated and overrun by grazing cattle who were left on their own. The MacKenzie's knew they had their work cut out for them from the start. Nonetheless, in 1974, they made the move to Jackson, and a twenty-seven-year love affair with dude ranching began as owners of their own ranch.

Serves 6-8

4 cups boiling water 1 cup quick grits 1/4 cup diced, fire-roasted Hatch chilies Salt to taste	1. Bring the water to a boil and add the remaining ingredients. Stir to combine. 2. Reduce heat to simmer, stir again, and cook for five minutes. 3. Remove from the heat and serve.

★ MAPLE-GLAZED STICKY BUNS

Vista Verde Ranch, Steamboat Springs, Colorado

In 1928, Arthur "Daddy Art" and Salome Tufly moved to Clark from Grand Junction. The family purchased the Blair/Hay Homestead in 1933. It was Salome's sister Jennie, a Spanish teacher, who exclaimed "Vista Verde" when looking south from the Homestead cabin to the newly irrigated lush "green view" of the hay fields in what is now called Sunday pasture. The Tuflys grew hay and grazed cattle at the ranch.

The Tuflys' boy, Hollis, bought the ranch in 1958 from his parents. It was Hollis who built the Homestead cabin for his bride, Jean, that now sits in the pasture south of the main lodge. He and Orvel Bedell's father started dairy cow operations near each other in Clark and teamed up with their hay operations, so the young boys in both families were good friends. In 1968, the Steamboat Springs Ski area opened. Hollis saw an opportunity for tourism income and started the first hunting, fishing, horseback riding, and pack trips.

Frank and Winton Brophy purchased the ranch in 1975, after having left the East Coast in search of a family lodge at the base of a ski resort. Not finding what they were looking for, and discovering the concept of dude ranching, they ended up purchasing Vista Verde. Frank and Winton are responsible for turning Vista Verde into a full-scale dude ranch. The Brophys built and named many of the cabins used today. They have all been remodeled several times since then, but the Brophys got the ball rolling to be sure. The Brophys used to entertain their guests in the Main Lodge that stood where the parlor stands today. Frank was looking to expand the season and make the ranch more of a multi-season operation, so in 1978, employees Mark and Brenda Weir started the winter ski program at Vista Verde.

John and Susanne Munn purchased Vista Verde in 1991, with a dream and a vision for retiring to the quiet life of dude ranching. John had been deeply involved in the auto industry, and then he owned Wheel Horse Corporation before selling it to Toro. The Munns did a complete ranch make over and brought in Bill Backer, and he has overseen every new project since. During the makeover, every cabin was gutted and remodeled, a new Lodge was built, and a new barn replaced the historic old barn. Suzanne's love of gardening was the ticket for a full landscaping plan to be put into play.

John's love of good food and wine spurred the shift of the culinary program to a focus on gourmet and creative food and wine. The multi-sport aspect of the ranch was enhanced with the addition of a mountain bike program, photography workshops, wine tastings, and horsemanship clinics. During the Munn's time at the ranch, the coveted Mobil 4-star ranking was awarded year after year. Many of the staff who John and Suzanne brought in during their time as owners continue at the ranch today, always working toward "betterness," which has been one of John's challenges over the years

In 2006, Jerry and Peggy Throgmartin became the next stewards of Vista Verde. Originally wanting a private ranch, their plans shifted when they found Vista Verde. Realizing the great gift they would have to share with others, they moved forward and jumped into dude ranching with both feet. With great enthusiasm for continuing the direction the ranch had been headed, they invested in a new indoor riding arena, a beautiful Great Room addition tied in with a remodel of the existing Lodge, remodels on a majority of the cabins, an addition of a swimming pool, and a totally new Kid's Hut.

In December 2016, the ranch came under the ownership of Laura and Chris Jones and their family. They are committed to continuing the tradition of providing a compelling dude ranch experience that is authentic, while still being luxurious, and at the end of the day connects their guests' hearts with home and continues what was started so many years ago.

When the snow is falling outside this ranch and people enjoy playing in it, it's wonderful to go inside and curl up in front of the fire with a yummy treat. This a ranch favorite!

Makes 24

Danish dough, one sheet, 17" x 25" 4 sticks unsalted butter, whipped 1 tablespoon ground cinnamon 8 tablespoons sugar 1 cup pecans, chopped 1 cup maple syrup 1 stick butter, melted	1. If the dough is frozen, allow it to warm slightly, but not too much. If it's too soft, it will be difficult to roll; if it's too frozen, it will crack. 2. Whip the butter in a mixer with a paddle attachment until very soft and spreadable. Spread the butter evenly over the entire surface of the dough with a spatula. 3. Combine the sugar and cinnamon in a bowl and sprinkle over the entire surface of the dough. 4. Tightly roll the dough evenly into a log. Wrap the dough first in plastic wrap and then in foil. Refrigerate overnight to set up. 5. The next day, combine the pecans, maple and melted butter in a bowl and spread on the bottom of a baking pan, then preheat the oven to 350°F. Remove the rolls from the refrigerator, remove the foil and plastic, slice into 24 pieces, and arrange in the baking pan. 6. Bake the rolls for 12 minutes, then rotate the pans and bake another 12 minutes until done. Remove from oven and allow to cool on a rack. 7. Turn out onto a platter to serve.

★ MONKEY BREAD

Red Rock Ranch, Kelly, Wyoming

According to the ranch, "In 2024, monkey bread became a delicious addition to the breakfast ride at Red Rock Ranch. This yummy, pull apart bread combines several tiny balls of dough coated in butter, cinnamon, and sugar. Drizzle this amazing breakfast treat with vanilla icing and serve pull apart style. Imagine yourself as you just rode to Crystal Creek and now are standing in line to eat a delicious breakfast. The campfire is bright and warm, and the delicious candy bacon and green chili grits are all ready to serve up."

Serves 8–10

1 1/2 cups whole milk, warmed to about 110°F

2 1/4 teaspoons platinum yeast from Red Star

1/4 cup granulated sugar

2 large eggs, room temperature

5 tablespoons unsalted butter, melted and slightly cooled

1 teaspoon salt

5 cups flour

Filling

12 tablespoons unsalted butter, divided

1 1/4 cups granulated sugar

1 tablespoon ground cinnamon

2/3 cup packed brown sugar

1 teaspoon pure vanilla extract

1. To make the dough, whisk the warm milk, yeast, and sugar together in a mixing bowl. Either stir by hand or use a stand mixer fitted with a dough hook or paddle attachment. Cover and allow to sit for 5 minutes.

2. Add the eggs, butter, salt, and 1 cup of the flour. Beat on low speed for 30 seconds, scrape down the sides of the bowl with a silicone spatula, then add the remaining flour. Beat on medium speed until the dough comes together and pulls away from the sides of the bowl, about 2 minutes.

3. Knead the dough with the mixer and beat for an additional 5–7 full minutes or knead by hand on a lightly floured surface for 5–7 full minutes. If the dough becomes too sticky during the kneading process, sprinkle 1 teaspoon of flour at a time on the dough or on the work surface/in the bowl to make a soft, slightly tacky dough. Do not add more flour than you need because you do not want a dry dough. After kneading, the dough should still feel a little soft. Poke it with your finger—if it slowly bounces back, your dough is ready to rise.

4. First rise: Lightly grease a large bowl with oil or nonstick spray. Place the dough in the bowl, turning it to coat all sides in the oil. Cover the bowl with aluminum foil, plastic wrap, or a clean kitchen towel. Allow the dough to rise in a relatively warm environment for 1–2 hours or until double in size.

5. Generously grease a 10–12-cup Bundt pan with butter or nonstick spray. (Nonstick spray is best for this recipe.)

6. Prepare the coating by melting 1/2 cup of unsalted butter in a medium bowl.

7. Mix granulated sugar and cinnamon together in another medium bowl.

8. When the dough is ready, punch it down to release the air. Working one at a time, take small pieces of dough and roll into balls (about 1.25 inches in diameter each). You will need 40–45 balls total, so be modest with their size. Dip each ball, one by one, in the melted butter and then generously roll in the cinnamon-sugar mixture to coat them. You may need more cinnamon-sugar depending on how heavy each ball is coated. Arrange the balls in the Bundt pan one at a time.

9. Cover the pan with a clean kitchen towel and allow the shaped monkey bread to rest for 20 minutes. The balls will slightly rise during this time.

10. Adjust oven rack to a lower position and preheat oven to 350°. (It's best to bake the monkey bread toward the bottom of the oven so the top doesn't burn.)

11. Finish the coating by melting remaining 1/4 cup butter and then whisk in the brown sugar and vanilla extract. Pour evenly all over the shaped monkey bread.

12. Bake for 35–45 minutes or until golden brown on top. Cover loosely with foil if the top is browning too quickly. Cool for 5–10 minutes, then invert onto a large serving plate or cake stand.

Notes

Freezing Instructions: Prepare recipe through step four. After dough rises, punch it down to release the air, then roll into 40–45 small balls as directed in step 8. Do not coat the balls. Place shaped dough balls on a baking sheet, then refrigerate for thirty minutes. Once cold, the dough balls won't stick together anymore. Place them in a freezer bag or freezer-friendly container, then freeze for up to three months. Thaw dough balls in the refrigerator or at room temperature, prepare the coating and Bundt pan, then coat the dough balls as instructed in step 6. Continue with the recipe.

Overnight Instructions: Prepare the recipe through step 3. Cover the dough tightly and refrigerate for up to about fifteen hours. At least three hours before you serve the monkey bread the next day, remove the dough from the refrigerator, keep covered, and allow to rise on the counter for about 1 to 2 hours. Continue with step 5.

Vanilla Icing
Makes 1/2 Cup

1 cup confectioners' sugar

3 tablespoons whole milk, room temperature

1/2 teaspoon pure vanilla extract

1. To make the icing, whisk all of the icing ingredients together.

2. Drizzle over monkey bread. Cut the bread into generous slices or let everyone pick off the gooey pieces themselves. That's the fun of this treat! Monkey bread tastes best served on the same day. Cover leftovers tightly and store at room temperature for one day and in the refrigerator for up to four days.

★ TILLIE'S CINNAMON ROLLS

Sylvan Dale Ranch, Loveland, Colorado

In the early 1900s, Mr. and Mrs. Frend Neville owned a small cattle ranch at the mouth of the Big Thompson River. Wealthy doctors from St Louis came to the area to hunt deer and liked it so much they wanted to bring their families. So, the Nevilles built some cabins and a lodge along the river and planted apple trees in the yard. Years later, the facilities were sold to Cotner College, a Christian Church school in Lincoln, Nebraska. But during the Depression of the '30s, Cotner College closed and Sylvan Dale was leased out as a youth camp.

Maurice Jessup, then a college kid in Oklahoma, overheard a conversation about the ranch and asked for a summer job. He hitchhiked to Loveland and caught a ride with the mail carrier. He was overwhelmed with the beauty of the mountains and the rushing water and immediately told Camp Director JB Weldon, "You know, I just love this place. Someday I'm going to own Sylvan Dale." That was in 1934. Twelve years later, the ranch was for sale, and Maurice Jessup was in the Army Air Corps. He received special permission to go and bid on the property. After scratching his bid on a piece of paper, he and his wife Mayme "Tillie" were awarded the 125-acre run-down property. He called her "Tillie" after a 1930s comic strip called, Tillie the Toiler.

Through a lifetime of hopes and dreams solidly based on faith, dedication, and hard work, the Jessups and their two children, David and Susan, increased the 125-acre ranch to a 3,200-acre working guest ranch. Grandnieces Tammy and Roseland recalled, "The highlight of all the wonderful food was the anticipation of devouring Aunt Mayme's delicious Cinnamon Rolls."

Makes 8

- 1 1/2 packages dry yeast (3 1/4 teaspoons)
- 1/4 cup warm water
- 1 cup milk
- 1/3 cup sugar
- 1 stick butter
- 1 1/2 teaspoons salt
- 1 egg, beaten
- 4–5 cups all-purpose flour

Filling

- 1 stick butter, melted
- 1 cup sugar
- 1 tablespoon cinnamon
- 1 cup raisins, optional

1. Place the yeast in a large bowl, add the warm water, and stir dissolve. Allow to sit for about 10 minutes. Set aside.
2. Scald the milk in a saucepan. Remove from heat, add the sugar and salt, then stir to dissolve. Add the butter and let it soften and melt and allow to cool down until warm.
3. Place 1 cup of flour in a large mixing bowl and add the dissolved yeast and beaten egg. Add the milk mixture and beat with a mixer for about 1–2 minutes until blended. Add 3 more cups of flour, one at a time, and beat again 1–2 minutes until smooth after each addition. With the third cup of flour, beat well. With the fourth cup of flour, beat as best you can since the dough will be thick. Clean the beaters and scrape down the bowl, then dump onto a lightly floured surface. Flour your hands and knead the dough, adding a small amount of flour as needed to handle the dough. Knead until elastic and smooth.
4. Place the dough in a lightly oiled bowl and cover with a clean cloth. Let rise in a warm place for 1 1/2 hours.
5. Press down the dough and dump it back onto a floured surface. Roll dough into a rectangular shape, about 1-inch thick.
6. Brush generously with melted butter. Spread a good layer of cinnamon sugar to 1 inch from the edges. Sprinkle with raisins, if using.
7. Roll up tightly, like a jelly roll, starting with the longer side. Seal the seam by pinching the edge of the rest of the roll.
8. Using sharp scissors or a piece of thread or string and cut into 1 to 1 1/2 inches thick slices. Place one slice in an 8- to 9-inch rounded, greased pan. Place one slice in the middle and the others around it. Press the rolls so they are even. Cover with a clean cloth and let rise for about another hour.
9. Bake on the middle rack of a pre-heated 350°F for 15–20 minutes until golden brown around the edges.

Orange Icing
Makes About 1 Cup

- 2 cups powdered sugar
- 1 tablespoon butter, melted
- 1/2 teaspoon vanilla
- 2–4 tablespoons milk
- 2–3 teaspoons grated orange peel

1. Place the powdered sugar, butter, and vanilla in a medium bowl. Stir in enough milk or cream to create a thick and hardly-able to stir mixture. Stir in orange zest.
2. Spread over warm rolls as soon as they are plated so the icing can melt and run into the rolls.

★ CHEDDAR BREAD
Flathead Lake Lodge, Bigfork, Montana

In 1932, a boys' camp called Flathead Recreation Ranch was built on the shores of Flathead Lake in Bigfork, Montana. The Main Lodge and the South Lodge were both built in the 1930s. Les Averill acquired the camp after returning home from WWII in 1945. Les, or Grandpa, as we call him, created a concept and philosophy at Flathead Lake Lodge that has successfully survived more than seventy-five years of dramatic changes in travel and vacation trends. And while transportation options, technology, and life has changed since 1945, the Averill family's idea of an authentic and memorable family vacation, filled with welcome and genuine hospitality, has remained the same. Doug and Maureen were the second generation to run the ranch, and today their oldest son, Chase, is at the helm with his wife Kate.

This ranch recipe started out as a basic white bread, but Maureen decided to add shredded and chunks of cheddar cheese to the dough. She chose this recipe because, "it was simple, and I had never cooked for two hundred people!"

Makes 3 loaves

- 2 1/2 cups, plus 2 tablespoons milk
- 1/3 cup water, plus 2 teaspoons
- 1/3 cup, plus 2 teaspoons white sugar
- 1 tablespoon salt
- 4 1/2 cups cheddar cheese, shredded
- 3 tablespoons butter
- 1 tablespoon yeast
- 8 1/4 cups flour

1. Heat milk, water, sugar, salt, half the cheese, and butter to 115–120°F.
2. Add yeast to mixture (look for bubbles to make sure yeast is active). Add half the flour and mix well. Add the remaining cheese and flour to form a supple dough.
3. Cover and allow to rise until it doubles or about an hour. Gently deflate dough and shape. Cover and allow to rise again until it doubles.
4. Bake at 350°F for 30–90 minutes. Allow to cool before slicing.

★ THE CHUCK WAGON ★

With so many cattle drives from the 1860s to the 1880s it became harder and harder to feed the ten to twenty men who tended the cattle. That's when a former Texas Ranger and cattle rancher came up with the chuck wagon.

The chuck wagon was in the invention of Charles Goodnight who was a Texas Ranger turned cattle rancher in Texas in the 1860s. In 1866 he and fellow rancher, Oliver Loving, created the Goodnight-Loving Trail through to move cattle. It originally ran from Texas, through New Mexico, Colorado, Wyoming, and into Montana Territory. Loving was killed in 1867 but Goodnight went on to expand the trail into Wyoming. In 1876 he entered into a partnership with Cornelia and John Adair to begin the JA Ranch in Palo Duro Canyon, Texas.

During Goodnight's cattle drives he saw the need for a way to feed the cowboys so he modified an army surplus Studebaker wagon. He strapped a box on the back and fitted it with cooking supplies like pots, utensils, staples, and more.

The invention changed the experience of the cattle drive for the cowboys on the trail. They also had the added benefit of the cookie, who ran the chuck wagon. He not only provided them meals, but was their doctor, seamstress, and confidant. They were paid $20-$30 a month and were affectionately called names like Belly-cheater, greasy belly, gut robber, Cookie, Sallie, Coosie, Beef-trust, Dog face, Dutch, Beans, Punk, Grease-pot and Whistle-berry. Most chuck wagon cooks didn't use recipes because they just knew how to cook. Some were cooks during the Civil War and others learned along the way.

Staples on the chuck wagon were things that traveled well and didn't spoil. The list included flour, sourdough, salt, brown sugar, beans, rice, cornmeal, dried apples and peaches, backing powder, baking soda, coffee, and "airtights," which were canned goods. Airtights included tomatoes, corn, and a gallon of syrup, which was usually molasses or sorghum. While fresh beef was the main meat, wild game and fish were sometimes available along the trail and during roundups. Bacon was used to fry everything, but also served as the main meat when supplies ran low.

Sometimes the cowboys were treated dessert and it usually consisted of cobbler, rehydrated fruit, or fruit pudding. Eggs were rare since they broke so easily, but sometimes the cook and cowboy traded local homesteaders for some.

★ HIGH ALTITUDE CORN BREAD

Drowsy Water Ranch, Granby, Colorado

Deane "Pop" Glessner is the founding father of Drowsy Water Ranch when he started it in the 1936 as a working ranch raising Saddlebred horses and Hereford cattle. He and his wife Lillian began operating it as a dude ranch in the 1940s until his death in the 1950s. Most guests arrived by Amtrak train and enjoyed a stay "out West." Lillian kept the ranch but needed help, so her daughter Barbara, along with her husband Dr. Thomas Jacques, managed the ranch, but both lived in Denver. Barabra said, "We plunged in up to our necks in 1954 after my stepfather died."

During the 1960s and into the 1970s, the ranch changed hands a few times before landing with Ken and Randy Sue Fosha, who bought it in the 1970s. They shared this. "We've been here for more than forty years, and we know the trails, the dust, and the horses like the back of our hands. We've fallen in love with the ranch and with the business. Many times, families who meet for the first time at the ranch become lifelong friends."

Makes 1 pan

1/2 cup flour	1. Combine dry ingredients in a small bowl.
1/2 cup cornmeal	2. In a separate bowl combine buttermilk, butter, and eggs. Mix together, then the dry ingredients and fold in the corn.
2 tablespoons sugar	
1 teaspoon baking powder	
1/4 teaspoon kosher salt	3. Pour into a greased 9 x 13-inch pan and bake at 400°F for 25 minutes.
1/2 cup buttermilk	
3 tablespoons butter, melted and cooled	
1 egg	
1/2 cup frozen corn, thawed	

★ BREAKFAST RIDE RANCH CANDY BACON

Red Rock Ranch, Kelly, Wyoming

Serves 4-6

1/4 teaspoon cayenne pepper
1/4 cup brown sugar
1 pound thick bacon
1/4 cup maple syrup

1. Combine the cayenne pepper and sugar in a deep bowl and combine.
2. Add the bacon and toss to evenly coat.
3. Lay bacon strips flat on a prepared sheet pan and bake at 375°F for 15 minutes.
4. Drizzle maple syrup over bacon and bake again for 5 minutes. It can be finished in a Dutch oven over a fire just like their chef does at the breakfast ride on the ranch.

CHAPTER TWO

APPETIZERS, SOUPS & SALADS

★ GRILLED SHRIMP COCKTAIL

Rancho del al Osa, Sasabe, Arizona

Rancho de la Osa is a unique convergence of Indian, Spanish, Mexican, ranching, political, and Hollywood/celebrity history. The ranch headquarters was originally a village for Tohono O'Odham (once called Papago) Indians and possibly the Hohokam. Many artifacts, including metates and pottery shards have been found and continue to be unearthed. Rancho de la Osa boasts Arizona's oldest continually used building that was built at the Tohono O'Odham village in 1722 by Jesuit missionaries who had traveled with Father Kino, who died in 1711. The building was a mission outpost which served as a place of worship, a trading post, and an inn for travelers. Today it is used for special events and ranch gatherings. The ranch was part of the original 1812 Ortiz Brothers Spanish land grant. With Mexican independence from Spain in 1812, the ranch became a part of Mexico, and in 1916, Pancho Villa raided and attempted to take Rancho de la Osa. A cannon ball from that attack was found embedded in the adobe wall of the hacienda and is on display today.

In the late 1800s, the ranch was bought by cattle baron Colonel William Sturgis, who built the great *hacienda,* which was finished in 1889. The ranch had become part of the United States, following the Gadsden Purchase of 1853. The adjacent Buenos Aires Federal Wildlife Refuge restored its own 130,000 acres to the pre-1880s great grasslands of Southern Arizona. In 1924, Louisa Wetherill, a noted Navajo historian and archeologist, came to the area and the ranch looking for a "lost" tribe of Navajo. They did not find the tribe but found the perfect place to build a dude ranch. Rancho de la Osa opened to guests on Thanksgiving 1924. Tom Mix was an early and regular guest to the ranch. Caesar Romero, Joan Crawford, Margaret Mitchell, and Zane Gray were also guests. John Wayne was a frequent guest and had a favorite room that is still in use today.

The historic dining room at Rancho de la Osa has been hosting dude ranch guests for mealtimes for over a century after it opened as Hacienda de la Osa in 1924. The ranch's *hacienda* was completed in 1887, while the ranch was a cattle ranch owned by Colonel William S. Sturges. He spared no expense finishing the Spanish-style hacienda, which featured wood floors, stained-glass windows, and ten acres of gardens. It was noted as "one of the most remarkable structures in the territory" and remained a large cattle ranch with headquarters where the ranch buildings remain today.

Serves 4

16–20 large shrimp

3/4 cup avocado oil

1/4 cup olive or vegetable oil

4 tablespoons butter, melted

1 tablespoon crushed red pepper flakes

1 tablespoon freshly coarse-ground pepper

1 teaspoon cumin

1 tablespoon soy sauce

1 teaspoon powdered mustard

1 tablespoon kosher salt

Lemon wedges, for serving

Cocktail sauce, for serving

1. Preheat the grill to high heat.
2. Peel and de-vein the largest shrimp that you want, using about 16–20, leaving on the tails. Drain and dry the shrimp and place them in a bowl.
3. Marinate the shrimp in the oil, crushed red pepper flakes, black pepper, cumin, soy sauce, mustard (wet can be used), and kosher salt. Toss all these ingredients with the shrimp in a large bowl. The shrimp do not need to marinate very long because the flavor comes from the high temperature while cooking.
4. Drain off the excess oil and carefully place the shrimp on the hot grill from back to front, leaving lots of space. Cooking time will vary depending on the size of the shrimp—larger shrimp will typically be about 1 minute per side. There should be nice char marks, and the shrimp will be about 80% cooked.
5. Pull them off the grill and let cool to room temperature, then put in a container and in the refrigerator until you want to serve. Serve on a large platter with lemon wedges and cocktail sauce. Rancho del al Osa adds fresh horseradish and lime juice to cocktail sauce, which is always a big hit at the ranch.

APPETIZERS, SOUP & SALADS | 21

★ RANCHO DE LA OSA OQUITOA COCKTAIL ★

Lois Ballenger Arthur was a frequent guest at Rancho de la Osa in the 1920s, when the ranch was called Hacienda de la Osa and was in its early years as a guest ranch. She described her travels through Sonora, Mexico, in her memoirs called *Mesquite & Mescal from 1926 to 1933*. In it she wrote, "For a desert thirst, there is no drink after water as refreshing as wild orange juice sweetened with a bit of honey and a dash of tequila; an Oquitoa cocktail." The town of Oquitoa is where she first tried the Oquitoa Cocktail, described to be used with the local mescal maguey. For regional flavor, this cocktail should be made with bacanora, the mescal variety from Sonora. For a less smokey flavor, reposado tequila is a delicious alternative.

Serves 1

2 ounces Bacanora or reposado tequila for a less smokey flavor 1/2 honey syrup Fresh squeezed orange juice Tajin or salt and orange or lime slice, garnish	1. Prepare glassware: rim with tajin or salt and add ice cubes. 2. Combine tequila and honey syrup in a shaker with ice. 3. Shake and strain into glass. 4. Top with fresh squeezed orange juice.

Honey Syrup

1/2 cup honey 1 cup water	1. Combine equal parts honey and water in a small pot over medium heat to dissolve the honey. 2. Allow to cool before using.

★ CARAMELIZED CARROT SOUP

Vista Verde Ranch, Steamboat Springs, Colorado

The chef is always creating new recipes at the ranch and guests enjoy the variety. Per the chef, "The quality of this soup depends entirely on the quality of the carrots that go into it, so use the highest quality carrots you can find. Carrot cores, rich in calcium, can add a bitter taste and unpleasant texture to this delicate soup, so we always remove them. It's an optional step; however, you can try the soup both ways and compare. Add a swirl of coconut cream and a few sprigs of tarragon in the final step to enhance the inherent sweetness of the carrots. Shredded young coconut is another favorite garnish of ours." *See the Maple-Glazed Sticky Buns recipe for the history of the ranch.*

Serves 6

- 5 cups carrots, peeled
- 1 1/8 cups water
- 1 1/4 teaspoons salt
- 3/8 teaspoon baking soda
- 1 stick butter
- 2 1/2 cups carrots juice
- 3 1/2 tablespoons butter
- Salt, to taste
- Swirl coconut cream, optional

1. Cut the carrots into 2-inch-long pieces. Remove the cores if you like.
2. Place the carrots, baking soda, and salt in a steamer and cook over boiling water until tender or about 20 minutes.
3. Place the carrots in a bowl and add the stick of butter, then blend into a smooth puree. Pass the puree through a sieve to remove any remaining pieces.
4. Place the carrot juice in a medium-sized stock pot and bring to a boil. Once it boils, strain it through a fine sieve.
5. Add the carrot puree and a small amount of water, if necessary, to thin the soup to a desired consistency. Add the remaining butter and blend the soup with an immersion blender until the butter has melted.
6. Season and serve warm. If using coconut cream, swirl around the top.

★ CEDAR PLANK WILD MUSHROOMS

Lone Mountain Ranch, Big Sky, Montana

Lone Mountain Ranch was first homesteaded by Clarence Lytle in 1915 as a working cattle and hay cutting ranch. Clarence and his brother William built many of the original structures on the ranch including Meadowlark Cabin—which still welcomes guests today—barns, corrals, and fence lines. In 1927, he sold the ranch to Chicago paper mill tycoon, J. Fred Butler, who spared no expense in building the ultimate vacation destination for his family. The Butlers built many of the existing lodgepole guest cabins and named the property the B-K Ranch. In the 1930s, the younger generation of Butlers opened the ranch to friends and guests visiting from back East. "Dudes" rode horses, panned for gold, fished, trapped, collected wildflowers, and enjoyed meals cooked by campfire. Guests flocked to the ranch to fulfill their cowboy ambitions, and as they do today, discovered an authentic experience that is true to nature.

After World War II, the ranch took on new purposes. For a few summers, it was used as a boys' camp—a place for young men to ride, fish, camp, and hunt while exploring the wilds of Montana.

Later, the ranch became home to a logging operation, and dozens of families took up residence in the old cabins and temporary tar paper houses. To accommodate all the children living on the ranch, the B-K Lodge was converted into a schoolhouse.

In 1955, the loggers left, and the ranch went back to welcoming guests in the tradition of Western hospitality. The property earned the name we still know it by today—Lone Mountain Ranch—and became a successful hunting and fishing camp for visitors seeking a true Montana experience. An old brochure referred to the property's "hundreds of white-faced cattle," part of the cattle ranching business the owners kept in the low seasons. Much like today, guests were greeted in Bozeman and brought back to the ranch for a week of horseback riding and other adventures.

In 1977, Bob and Vivian Schaap bought Lone Mountain Ranch with a dream to turn it into one of the world's premier cross country ski destinations. Over the course of thirty years, the Schaaps established and refined a year-round guest experience that celebrated the good things in life—and the very best of Montana. Guests from around the world became regular faces at the ranch, where generations of families created lasting memories.

The cedar plank smoked mushrooms dish at Lone Mountain Ranch's Horn and Cantle pays homage to the rich tradition of ranch foraging culture. By using the freshest sourced mushrooms and the age-old technique of cedar plank smoking, this dish captures the earthy, natural flavors reminiscent of foraging in the wild. It's a culinary celebration of the ranch's connection to the land, offering a taste of the simple yet profound ingredients found in its natural surroundings.

Serves 2–4

2 pounds lion's mane, oyster, cremini, chestnut, or your favorite mushrooms	1. Sear mushrooms on high heat in a large cast iron skillet for about 15–20 minutes or until golden and slightly firm.
1 teaspoon fresh garlic, minced	2. Add the garlic and shallots and deglaze with white wine. Add butter, parsley, and lemon juice.
1 teaspoon shallots, minced	
1 ounce white wine	
Fresh parsley, chopped	3. Spread chevre in your chosen serving vessel, plate mushrooms, then garnish with lemon zest and more parsley. While this dish is served as an appetizer at Horn and Cantle, it can also be a great side dish.
1 teaspoon unsalted butter	
1/2 cup soft Chevre	
1 lemon, zested and juiced	
Salt and pepper, to taste	

★ PARMESAN CUSTARD WITH GLAZED SPRING VEGETABLES

Vista Verde Ranch, Steamboat Springs, Colorado

The ranch typically shares recipes that are fairly accessible for all types of home cooks. However, Chef Jonathon wanted to share this recipe and give adventurous cooks a culinary challenge. *See the Maple-Glazed Sticky Buns recipe for the history of the ranch.*

Serves 6

2/3 cup cream

2/3 cup whole milk

3 1/2 ounces Parmesan, cut into 1/2-inch pieces

2 eggs

1 egg yolk

1/2 teaspoon kosher salt

1/8 teaspoon white pepper

Butter for molds

18 large asparagus spears

1 cup shelled English peas

1 cup fava beans

18 small morel mushrooms, cleaned

1 shallot, peeled and sliced into rings

3 tablespoons butter

Kosher salt and fresh cracked black pepper, to taste

Chive blossoms or other edible flowers, optional

1. Bring cream, milk, and cheese to simmer in a small sauce pot. Turn off the heat, cover, and let steep for 45 minutes.
2. Heat oven to 250°F.
3. In a medium bowl, whisk eggs and yolk.
4. Strain cream, bring to boil, then temper into egg mixture. Whisk in salt and pepper.
5. Butter six 3-ounce timbale molds and fill 2/3 full with custard, place in baking dish, then add enough hot water to the pan to come halfway up the sides of the timbale molds.
6. Cover with foil and bake for 30 minutes.
7. After 30 minutes, carefully remove foil and jiggle one of the center molds. Custards should jiggle like Jello and give the impression that the custard is set.
8. Once set, CAREFULLY remove custards from the oven, remove foil, and set aside until needed.
9. Trim the top 1–1 1/2-inch of asparagus nibble on stalks.
10. Bring a medium sauce pot filled with water and salted (almost like the ocean) to a boil. Blanch asparagus for 3 minutes in an ice bath and then remove.
11. In the same water, blanch peas for 5 minutes, then shock in an ice bath.
12. If using fava beans, remove beans from the pod, blanch 5 minutes, then shock in an ice bath. Once cool, using a sharp paring knife, make a small incision in the husk and pinch the bean out. Set aside.
13. Heat a medium-sized sauté pan over medium heat. Add butter and about 1/4 cup water. Once butter is melted and the mixture is boiling, add veggies and cover until the liquid returns to simmer. At that point, season lightly with kosher and gently toss veggies. Let cook until the water has evaporated and the butter has glazed the veggies.
14. To serve: Run a thin-bladed knife around the edge of the custard, turn it out onto a plate, and carefully spoon some of the veggies around. Serve immediately.

★ CHILLED CORN SOUP

Vista Verde Ranch, Steamboat Springs, Colorado

This is another ranch guest favorite during the summertime, which is the perfect time of the year for chilled soups. The chef created this recipe just in time for the Olathe corn to be coming into season. Olathe corn and corn in general isn't a major crop in most of Colorado, but there is a small area in the state where it has been produced with renowned success. *See the Maple-Glazed Sticky Buns recipe for the history of the ranch.*

Serves 8

6 ears corn, shucked

3 cups buttermilk

1/2 cup basil leaves, plus more for garnish

6 scallion stalks, roughly chopped

1 tablespoon fresh lime juice, more to taste

2 fat garlic cloves, roughly chopped

Kosher salt, to taste

1/2 cup ice cubes

Radish slices, for garnish

Chives, thinly sliced, for garnish

Extra-virgin olive oil, for garnish

1. Slice kernels off the corncobs, making about 6–7 cups of kernels.

2. Discard cobs and place kernels in a blender. Add buttermilk, basil, scallions, lime juice, garlic, salt, and ice cubes to the blender and purée until very smooth. Strain mixture through a sieve, pressing down hard on the solids. Discard the leftover solids.

3. Chill the soup 2 hours until ready to serve. Serve soup garnished with radish slices, chives, and a drizzle of olive oil.

★ COWBOY COFFEE ★

While coffee was a staple in every camp, coffee beans weren't always available. Ingenious cookies learned to brew coffee with substitute beans, using cornmeal, barley, or wheat. Jonathan Sanford Ater lived in Texas in the late 1800s. He recalled, "Coffee was made from parched corn, okra, diced sweet potatoes, wheat, or rye."

Coffee and eggs sound good, right? How about eggs in your coffee? It's true—brewing a pot of coffee was much different back in the day. The grounds were cooked in a pot, with no filter or strainer. Adding eggshells to the pot was a way to keep the coffee grounds at the bottom.

W. H. Thomas, an 1870s Texas cowhand, remembered camp coffee: "One thing you could depend on at any time of the day or night, especially in the winter and that was the blackest coffee that can be made. I can just see the old coffee pot now, big enough to hold a couple gallons at a time, and a couple of egg shells floating around in it to settle the grounds. We never got but few eggs to eat and we always accused cookie of carrying the same egg shells around from year to year."

A cowboy named Charles Siringo turned his cowboy experiences into a book. He told his first tales in 1885, but then wrote an expanded version in 1919 called, *A Lone Star Cowboy*. He penned, "We always started the day's work at the first peep of day and never thought of eating a noon meal. Often it would be pitch dark when we arrived in camp, where a warm camp fire meal awaited us. These meals were made up of meat from a fat heifer calf, with corn bread, molasses, and black coffee. The Negro cook, who drove the mess-wagon, generally had two kinds of meat, the calf ribs broiled before the camp fire, and a large Dutch oven full of loin, sweet-breads, and heart mixed with flour gravy. For breakfast we often had pork and beans which had been simmering over hot coals all night. In those days, knives and forks were seldom used in the cow camps; each cowboy used his bowie knife or pocket knife to eat with."

Arbuckle's was synonymous with coffee to the cowboys. Up until the Civil War coffee was purchased green, roasted over the fire until just the right color, and then ground. Then it was boiled to make coffee. Two brothers changed all that in the 1860s.

John and Charles Arbuckle initiated a new concept in the coffee industry when they started selling roasted coffee in one-pound packages. The Arbuckle Brothers were able to roast a coffee that was a consistent fine quality product. It was also the first to be packaged in one-pound bags. Arbuckles' Ariosa blend became so popular in the Old West that most cowboys didn't even know that there was any other. The Arbuckle Brothers enjoyed immense success into the 20th Century and often made the papers.

★ ANN OLSON'S SPINACH SALAD WITH DRESSING

Nine Quarter Circle Ranch, Gallatin Gateway, Montana

Homesteaders settled the Nine Quarter Circle Ranch just outside Yellowstone National Park in the late 1800s as more people became drawn to the area. In 1912, the Butler family from Chicago consolidated early homesteads to create Nine Quarter Circle. The working horse ranch has welcomed travelers and introduced them to the ways of the West ever since. Guests can experience one family's strong commitment to a friendlier, simpler bygone era. It's the reason sturdy, timeless 1920s era buildings are still in use at the ranch today.

It's also why the Kelsey family began building a herd of exclusive horses, all bred, born, raised, and trained on the ranch, beginning in the 1950s. And it's why the many generations passing through the ranch have experienced the same genuine ranch customs of mealtime, work, and outdoor recreation.

Serves 8

- 2/3 cup sugar
- 1 teaspoon dry mustard
- 1 teaspoon paprika
- 1 teaspoon celery seed
- 1 teaspoon salt
- 1/3 cup vinegar
- 1 tablespoon lemon juice
- 1 teaspoon grated onion, optional
- 1/3 cup honey
- 1 cup salad oil
- 10 cups spinach
- Bacon crumbles, to taste
- 4 hard-boiled eggs, sliced

1. Mix all ingredients, except for oil, spinach, bacon, and eggs in a bowl.
2. Drizzle the oil into the bowl, then use a whisk or a mixer to emulsify and blend to a dressing consistency.
3. Place the spinach in a salad bowl. Crumble bacon over spinach and cut hard-boiled eggs into it. Add the dressing and toss.

★ BROCCOLI SALAD

Vista Verde Ranch, Steamboat Springs, Colorado

This is a perfect salad for a backyard cookout or a weekend picnic. It's a favorite summer lunch dish at the ranch when everyone comes in hungry from their adventures out on the trails. *See the Maple-Glazed Sticky Buns recipe for the history of the ranch.*

Serves 8

1/4 cup whole grain Dijon mustard

1/2 cup mayonnaise

1/2 cup crème fraiche or sour cream

1/4 cup granulated sugar

2 heads broccoli, cut into bite sized pieces

1/2 pound bacon, cooked and chopped

1 small red onion, diced

1 1/2 cups grated parmesan cheese

salt and pepper, to taste

1. In a small bowl, combine the mustard, mayo, crème fraiche, sugar, salt, and pepper and whisk together.
2. In a larger bowl, add remaining ingredients, then combine with mustard/mayo mixture and taste for seasoning. Adjust as needed. Refrigerate until ready to serve. Enjoy!

CHAPTER THREE

SIDES, VEGETABLES, SEASONINGS & SAUCES

★ FLATHEAD LAKE LODGE BEANS

Flathead Lake Lodge, Bigfork, Montana

This recipe was created when owner Doug fired the chef on a Monday and his wife, Maureen, had to produce beans for 200 people on Wednesday. She didn't have any dried beans, nor the time to soak and cook them, but she found cans of pork and beans and started dumping ingredients into them that she thought would make them not taste like "pork 'n beans." Her creation was a hit, and the ranch still serves them. However, you need to be creative like Maureen because there are not set measurements, only a list of ingredients. *See the Cheddar Bread recipe for the history of the ranch.*

Serves As Many As You Like

Canned pork & beans	1. Add as much of the ingredients as you like.
Molasses	2. Mix everything in a large bowl and stir to blend.
Honey	3. Bake the beans for 5 hours in a low oven at 250° to 275°F.
Brown Sugar	
Ketchup	
Soy Sauce	
Worcestershire	
Burned bacon, chopped	
Diced onion	
Dried tarragon	
Dried basil	
Dried rosemary	
Dried marjoram	
Dried thyme	
Dried oregano	
Cayenne	
Paprika	
Garlic, minced	
Chili Powder	
Onion Powder	
Ground Mustard	

★ MUSHROOM RISOTTO

Vista Verde Ranch, Steamboat Springs, Colorado

There is nothing like a warm and creamy bowl of risotto after a day of riding. *See the Maple-Glazed Sticky Buns recipe for the history of the ranch.*

Serves 2

- 1 stick butter
- 1/2 yellow onion, peeled and minced
- 2 cups carnaroli rice
- 1 cup dry white wine
- 1 quart vegetable stock, simmering
- 1/2 pound mushrooms, sliced
- 1/4 soy sauce
- 1 cup crème fraiche or sour cream or heavy cream
- 1/2 cup Parmesan cheese
- Salt, to taste

1. Melt the butter in a heavy bottomed pan on medium high heat. Add onions and sauté until the onions are translucent.
2. Add the rice and cook while stirring until a nutty smell develops. Deglaze the pan with white wine. Reduce the heat to low.
3. Cook the wine down until nearly dry while slowly stirring the rice.
4. Slowly add the vegetable stock a half cup at a time, while stirring the rice, waiting each time for the stock to nearly evaporate.
5. Meanwhile, in a separate sauté pan, sauté the mushrooms on high heat to sear slightly. Deglaze with soy sauce and immediately remove from the heat.
6. Check the rice for tenderness, season with salt and parmesan cheese, and finish by folding in the mushrooms and crème fraiche just before serving.
7. Risotto should be a bit loose and flow on the plate.

★ JALAPENO CHEDDAR POLENTA

Lone Mountain Ranch, Big Sky, Montana

For over a hundred years, Lone Mountain Ranch has been a symbol of the American West. They had a seat at the table for the early days of Yellowstone Park, the formation of the town of Big Sky, the evolution of ranching and logging in the Northern Rockies, and the preservation of Montana's spectacular wilderness. Ever since it was homesteaded in 1915, their story has had one consistent thread—warm and welcoming hospitality to all. Take a walk back through time to get a sense of Lone Mountain Ranch's roots and the real Montana.

This dish is served with their Bison Short Ribs (recipe on another page). *See the Cedar Plank Mushrooms for additional history of the ranch.*

Serves 4–6

6 cups water 2 cups heavy cream 2 cups yellow polenta 2 cups sharp white cheddar 5 fresh jalapenos, charred, deseeded, and small diced Fresh parsley, chopped, for garnish Salt and pepper, to taste	1. Place water and heavy cream into a large sauce pan and bring the liquids to a boil. 2. Whisk in the polenta in increments and continuously whisk slowly for about 15 minutes or until desired consistency. If the polenta is too thick, add more water. When this is achieved, fold in cheddar and jalapenos. Salt and pepper to taste. 3. Garnish with parsley and serve.

★ ORANGE BOURBON CARROTS

Flat Creek Ranch, Flat Creek, Wyoming

See the Pastina recipe for the history of the ranch.

Serves 8

1 quart orange juice 1 cup bourbon 1 tablespoon whole black peppercorns 2 bay leaves 5 sprigs fresh thyme 1 sprig fresh sage 3 sprigs fresh marjoram 16 rainbow carrots 1 tablespoon butter 1 tablespoon olive oil	1. Place the orange juice and bourbon in a sauce pan burn alcohol off by simmering or lighting the bourbon with a torch. Once the alcohol has burnt off, add peppercorn, bay leaves, thyme, sage, and marjoram. Reduce by two-thirds and strain the solids from the liquid and set aside. 2. Peel and trim the carrots. Place in a saucepan of boiling water and blanch for 4 minutes. Transfer into an ice bath to stop the cooking process. Set aside. 3. In a sauté pan melt butter and olive oil on medium high heat and add the blanched carrots. Cook until slightly browned or about 2 minutes on each side. Add the bourbon glaze and allow to reduce, about 4 minutes.

★ PASTINA

Flat Creek Ranch, Flat Creek, Wyoming

In 1873, future Flat Creek Ranch homesteader Cal Carrington was born as Enoch Julin in Sweden. At age five, Cal arrived in the U.S. in the custody of Swedish Mormon Missionaries bound for Utah. However, by 1889, Cal had enough of his Idahoan foster father and left home. Cal recalled, "When I was sixteen, and big enough, I beat the hell out of the sonovabitch and ran away."

In late July 1900, this lanky cowpoke signed on as the camp cook on an English aristocrat's hunting expedition into the mountains above Jackson Hole. After three months with sparse success, the hunting party spent its final night on the trail in a secluded meadow ten miles east of Jackson, Wyoming. Winding down the middle of the valley was a spring-fed stream called Flat Creek, which is where Flat Creek Ranch is today. Local legend has it that it was the perfect spot for Cal to hide his rustled horses. He recalled, "I could see the sheriff a' coming either way." He moved into an abandoned trapper's cabin at what would become Flat Creek Ranch.

Cal became a naturalized American citizen with the name Enoch Carrington in 1905 and swore, "I have behaved as a man of good moral character." Despite a questionable past, Cal was hired as an assistant forest ranger of the National Forest Service in Wyoming. About 1912, Cal went to work as a "head guide in charge of pack outfits" at the new Bar BC Ranch, that would become Jackson Hole's most celebrated dude ranch. Cal recalled, "I decided it was time to get respectable and go into dudin'."

It was the summer of 1917 when a Chicago newspaper heiress and social celebrity named Eleanor "Cissy" Patterson arrived in Jackson Hole on a horse-drawn wagon with her daughter Felicia and her French maid. Cissy was an accomplished horsewoman and a big game hunter who decided to stay. She was introduced as Countess Gizycka, a title she retained even though she was divorced from the philandering Russian count, Josef Gizycki.

Cal met Cissy and soon found themselves attracted to each other. Romantic evenings and long hunting trips ensued. Cissy left but came back the next summer and rented the White Grass Ranch and hired Cal to be her ranch manager. One day Cal and Cissy rode up to see Cal's secret place on upper Flat Creek. Her biographer wrote, "Cissy thought it the most perfect place she had ever seen." The following fall, Cal had the 141 acres surveyed. His aim was to make the ranch his homestead and thus gain title to own the land. The ranch is surrounded on all sides by the Bridger-Teton National Forest.

On March 3, 1920, when Cal officially established residence at the ranch and began clearing stumps and cutting logs. Within two years, he was running twenty-five cattle and horses. Cissy wrote her first newspaper story celebrating the election victory of an all-women slate of candidates in Jackson in 1920. By some accounts, it was Cissy who inspired the six Jackson women to run for office.

Two years later, while staying at Claridge's Hotel in London, Cissy wrote a letter of introduction for Cal to one of her Washington social acquaintances, the powerful Senator Francis E. Warren of Wyoming, who was chairman of the Senate Appropriations Committee. The letter asked Senator Warren to help Cal find his way through the Washington bureaucratic thicket so he could get Flat Creek Ranch as his homestead. In March, enroute back home from Europe, Cal spent several days in Washington lobbying. He delivered Cissy's letter to Senator Warren and visited the headquarters of the Forest Service. That December, Cal was granted a homestead patent.

In February 1923, Cal sold the ranch to Cissy, and the two remained close friends with Cal as her hunting guide for some years. Cissy expanded the ranch from Cal's original cabin into her own private guest ranch of six cabins, a barn, and a lodge. Sadly, in 1948, Cissy died and left the ranch to her niece Josephine Patterson Albright, who thought it was too remote to use. For the next four decades, she leased it out to a succession of trout fishing devotees, while keeping an eye on things from her own ranch in nearby Dubois, Wyoming. In 1986, Josephine donated Flat Creek Ranch to the Jackson Hole Land Trust to protect it. She put a permanent conservation easement on the land and included a proviso that her heirs would have first option to buy back the ranch at an appraised price following her death.

The ranch was bought back from the Land Trust in 1998 by Josephine's son, Joe Albright following Josephine's death. Joe and his wife Marcia Kunstel loved the area so much they moved to Wyoming to fix up the ranch, which had fallen into disrepair. They found a conservation-minded contractor named Porgy McClelland who recruited a crew willing to live part-time at the ranch during a lengthy renovation project. In 2001, Joe and Marcia opened Flat Creek Ranch as a dude ranch. In 2014, Joe Albright and Marcia retired from daily operations, and Trey and Shelby Scharp took over as general managers and were excited to continue the tradition of Flat Creek Ranch.

This recipe is served with their Cornish Hens *(recipe on another page.)*

Serves 8

2 pounds butternut squash	1. Peel and deseed your butternut squash and cut into planks. Bake on a sheet at 425°F for 50 minutes or until fork tender. Cool for about 10 minutes.
6 cups chicken stock	
6 cups beef stock	
2 cups dry Arici de Pepe	2. Combine cooked squash and chicken stock in a blender and blend until smooth. Salt to taste and set aside. Reserve about 1 cup and put in a squeeze bottle for garnish.
1/2 cup shredded Parmesan cheese	
1/2 cup shredded Pecorino cheese	
5 egg yolks	3. Bring beef broth to a boil in a large pot and cook Arici de Pepe for 9 minutes or until al dente.
Salt and pepper, to taste	
	4. Whisk in your butternut squash puree, shredded cheese, egg yolks, and salt and pepper to taste.

★ ROASTED ROOT VEGETABLES

Lone Mountain Ranch, Big Sky, Montana

This recipe is served at the ranch with the Bison Short Ribs (recipe on another page). *See the Bison Short Ribs recipe and the Cedar Plank Mushrooms recipe for the history of the ranch.*

Serves 2–4

3 parsnips
2 turnips
5 cups fresh brussels sprouts
2 large carrots
1 large red onion
Olive oil, for tossing
Salt and pepper, to taste
Unsalted butter and fresh herbs, optional

1. Peel and cut all vegetables into desired shapes. Keep in mind that the vegetables will cook at different times (carrots will take much longer to cook than onions). The chef suggests roasting each of the vegetables separately and letting them cool, mixing them, and then reheating them. Or cut them into sizes that will all finish cooking at the same time.
2. Regardless how they are cooked, toss the raw vegetables in a decent olive oil, season with salt and pepper, and roast in oven at 425°F for 10 minutes or until desired doneness. The chef suggests unsalted butter and fresh herbs to finish the dish.

★ SAUCE BORDELAISE

Lone Mountain Ranch, Big Sky, Montana

This sauce complements the ranch's broiled steaks. *See the Bison Short Ribs recipe and the Cedar Plank Mushrooms recipe for the history of the ranch.*

Makes about 3 1/2 cups

1 1/2 quarts Mirepoix (equal parts onion, celery, and carrots)
15 fresh whole garlic cloves, peeled
1 quart red wine
1/2 cup tomato paste
2 quarts demi-glace
1/4 cup each, fresh rosemary and parsley
Salt and pepper, to taste

1. Cook mirepoix and garlic in a saucepot at high heat until vegetables are cooked through and fond has formed on the bottom of the pan.
2. Deglaze with red wine while scraping fond from pan with wooden spoon. When the pan is almost dry, add tomato paste, demi-glace, and herbs.
3. Cook sauce at low simmer until reduced by one-third.
4. Let sauce cool overnight. Reheat and strain, season with salt and pepper to taste.

★ POTATO GRATIN

Lone Mountain Ranch, Big Sky, Montana

One of the signature items at their restaurant, Horn and Cantle, is broiled steaks to order. Home cooks can use an outdoor grill or sear the steak in a large cast iron pan and finish it in the oven. The chef suggests serving the steak at medium rare/medium 130° to 140°F. See the Cedar Plank Mushrooms recipe for the history of the ranch. They serve Sauce Bordelaise, grilled asparagus, and this dish with the steak.

Serves 6–8

- 2 large yellow onions, sliced
- 10 fresh garlic cloves, minced
- 1 pound blend shredded fontina, gruyere, cheddar, parmesan cheeses
- 3 pounds Yukon Gold potatoes
- 1 quart heavy cream

1. Caramelize onions and garlic in medium sauté pan on low heat. Let onions cool.
2. Place the cheeses in a mixing bowl and fold in the cooled onions.
3. Thinly slice potatoes with a knife or mandolin and soak in heavy cream for an hour, refrigerated. Drain the potatoes of excess cream.
4. Line a 2-inch roasting pan with parchment paper and spray with oil.
5. Start with a single layer of potatoes covering the bottom of the roasting pan, followed by a light layer of cheese and onion mixture. Repeat process until 1/4-inch from top of the pan. Cover with aluminum foil and cook in oven for 45 minutes at 350°F. Uncover and cook another 10–15 minutes, until the top of gratin is golden brown.
6. Let the gratin cool for 1 hour (if served too hot the gratin will slide apart and ruin all of the layers). Add more cheese to the top and broil until melted. This dish can also set overnight in refrigerator, then cut into portions, reheated, and served.

★ CHUCK WAGON COOKS ★

Being a chuck wagon cook in the Old West was a tough job. He only had certain ingredients to cook with, and sometimes had to deal with unruly cowhands. Here are three accounts of their lives.

You know the old saying "Never bring a knife to a gunfight"? Well, that's just what Frenchy the cookie should have remembered. John Baker was born a Texan in 1850, but he traveled to Wyoming, the Dakotas, and New Mexico on cattle drives. He remembered Frenchy: "The belly-cheater on the Holt outfit was a fellow called Frenchy and a top cookie. Frenchy and a fellow named Hinton got into it over Hinton digging into the chuck box which was against Frenchy's rule as it was with any good cookie. They did not want the waddies messing up the chuck box. Hinton seemed to get a kick out of seeing Frenchy get riled and would mess around the chuck box. "The evening that the fight took place Hinton walked past Frenchy and dove into the chuck box. Frenchy went after Hinton with a carving knife and Hinton drew his gun. Frenchy was hit several times and Hinton was cut in a number of places . . . Cookie kept diving in close and slashing, finally he drove the knife into Hinton's breast and they both went to the ground and died a few minutes later."

So, this guy lost his pants to a couple of cows . . . I bet you were waiting for the punchline. Well, there isn't one—this is a true story! The multitasking Julius McKinney was preparing the noonday meal, while also washing his clothes. Not wanting to be naked, he fashioned a shirt and pants from used corn sacks. After finishing up a pan of biscuit dough, he went to check his clothes. To his dismay, they were gone. Looking downriver he saw two cows chewing on his clothes. Texas waddy Bill Kellis reported, "These two bovines were noted as the worst chewers on the ranch." McKinney tried to chase the cows, but to no avail. Kellis noted, "He could never face the boys all dressed up in his corn sacks; they would razz him to death. Knowing that he could never be seen in the corn sack suit he determined to get away somehow, so he mounted one of the wagon mules and rode for San Angelo, fifty miles away, the nearest place at which he could purchase a shirt and pants."

Some of the belly-cheaters were a little rough around the edges, as Texas waddy E. L. remembered: "The belly-cheater would have chow ready before daylight in the morning. He would yell, 'come an' get yo'r hell,' about the break of day. Sometimes he would yell, 'washup snakes an' come to it.' When he yelled that we always calculated that he had a fair to middlin' dish of nourishment shaped up . . . The bread was sourdough gun wadding an' often we were treated to saddle blankets. You greeners call it griddle cakes." "Gun wadding" is cowboy slang for a loaf of light bread, according to Scott Gregory's book, *Sowbelly and Sourdough*. "Saddle blankets" or "griddle cakes" is the cowboy's name for large pancakes.

★ SAUSAGE, APPLE, AND PECAN QUINOA

Rancho de los Caballeros, Wickenburg, Arizona

See the Herb Crusted Pork Tenderloin recipe for the history of the ranch. This dish pairs with that recipe as well.

Serves 7

4 tablespoons butter	1. Melt the butter over medium heat and sauté the onion, carrot, celery, and garlic until softened.
1/3 cup diced yellow onion	
1/4 cup diced carrots,	
1/4 cup diced celery	2. Deglaze the pan with white wine.
3 cloves garlic, minced	3. Add the apple, quinoa, bay leaf, thyme, sage, apple cider vinegar, and chicken stock and cook on low heat until quinoa is tender and stock has been absorbed.
5 ounces white wine	
1 1/4 cups diced apple	
1 1/4 cups quinoa, tri-colored	
5 bay leaves	4. In another pan, fry the sausage until crispy.
2 sprigs thyme, dried	5. Add the cooked sausage and pecans to quinoa and stir until mixed. Season with salt.
5 sprigs sage, fresh	
1 tablespoon apple cider vinegar	6. Allow to cool and add parsley.
2 1/2 cups chicken stock	
5 ounces diced sausage	
Salt, to taste	
6 tablespoons pecans, chopped	
1/4 cup parsley	

CHAPTER FOUR

MAIN DISHES & ENTRÉES

★ BACON & BROWN BUTTER CAST-IRON TROUT

The Broadmoor's Ranch at Emerald Valley, Colorado Springs, Colorado

The idyllic setting of the Pikes Peak region and Colorado Springs was the location Spencer Penrose chose when he planned the Broadmoor. His goal was to operate the most luxurious hotel in the world, and his destination property included something for everyone—who had money. He created a golf course and offered boating and polo. The hotel's interior decorator, Charles Wesling of Philadelphia, emphatically stated in 1917 that "the Broadmoor hotel will be one of the most remarkable in the world." By 1920, Penrose was the envy of hotel menacross America.

Penrose wanted nothing but the best, so he hired a young Italian chef named Louis Stratta and ensured his waitstaff was trained to European standards of the day. Stratta believed in food both tasting good and being eye-appealing. He was thirty-two years old when the hotel opened and served as the Broadmoor's head chef and pastry chef for decades.

The Ranch at Emerald Valley is an adventure into the majesty of green wonderlands. It's a place in which to feel completely disconnected from the bustle of normal life and cocooned by the timeless beauty of nature. Gentle horses and skilled ranch hands welcome visitors into this hidden valley of lakes, lawns, and waterfalls, where serene wilderness blends with the Broadmoor's genuine, Western hospitality to create a place that celebrates the best of both worlds. It was built around authentic Rocky Mountain cabins and surrounded by over 100,000 acres of the Pike National Forest.

Serves 1

2 tablespoons butter	1. Season trout with salt and pepper. Begin by slowly browning the butter in a pan over medium heat. Once it has reached the smell of toasted hazelnuts, pull it off the heat and set aside.
1–2 tablespoons canola oil or oil of your choice	
7-ounce trout fillet	
Salt, to taste	2. Heat a cast iron skillet over medium to medium-high heat. Once hot, add the oil and then the fish, skin-side down.
Pepper, to taste	
2 pieces hickory smoked bacon, diced	3. Cook until firm, about 4 minutes and then flip and cook to desired doneness. Remove from heat and place on serving plate.
2 lemon slices	
1 pinch Italian parsley, chopped	
	4. Meanwhile, in a separate pan over medium-high heat, render the bacon until crisp. Drain the fat from the pan.
	5. Return bacon to the pan and add the brown butter and the lemon. Cook for 1 minute. Finish by pouring browned butter sauce over the trout and garnishing with chopped parsley.

★ HONEY GLAZED PORK ROAST

Tombstone Monument Ranch & Cattle Co., Tombstone, Arizona

This ranch was founded by German immigrants Herman and Mary Trappman in 1880 who began raising cattle. Their descendants, the Escapules, continued for three generations until the ranch was sold in the 1990s. Today, Criollo, "America's first cattle," are raised here. They were originally brought to North America in 1493 on Christopher Columbus's second voyage. Tombstone Monument Ranch & Cattle Company is a working cattle and guest ranch just outside the center of the West's most iconic cowboy town: Tombstone, Arizona. The ranch is surrounded by historic mines, hand dug wells, old railroad trestles, and ancient Indian petroglyphs. The ranch itself is built in the image of an Old West town. Guests can wake up in the Grand Hotel, the marshal's office, the blacksmith's, or even the jail.

This delicious dinner entree has become a staple in Tombstone Monument Ranch's weekly guest menu. Dude ranch guests dine family-style on a hearty menu after a day spent experiencing the Old West first hand and then can gather in the ranch's Western saloon after dinner for some live music or a round of Texas Hold 'Em.

Serves 2–4

2-pound pork loin 1 tablespoon olive oil Equal parts paprika, seasoned salt, and garlic powder, to taste 1 1/2 cups water Honey garlic glaze (recipe follows)	1. Dry pork loin and rub with olive oil, then generously rub with the paprika, seasoned salt, and garlic. 2. Place the pork in a roasting pan and add the water. 3. Roast for 10 minutes at 425°F, then reduce temperature to 375°F for 50 minutes or until internal temperature reaches 145°F. Drain juice to make a gravy for mashed potatoes served as a side. 4. Cover with foil and let rest for 10 minutes before thinly slicing to serve.

Honey Garlic Glaze

2 tablespoons butter 2 tablespoons garlic, minced (about 4 cloves) 1/4 cup soy sauce 1/2 cup honey	1. Melt butter in a saucepan over medium heat and add the garlic. Cook garlic until it becomes soft, add the soy sauce and honey and bring to a boil over medium high heat until the sauce starts to thicken. 2. Pour over sliced pork when ready to serve. "This sauce is great on chicken as well."

MAIN DISHES & ENTRÉES | 49

★ HERB CRUSTED PORK TENDERLOIN

Rancho de los Caballeros, Wickenburg, Arizona

Dallas Gant, Sr., C.L. Maguire, and Belford Howard, along with their wives, began their journey of opening a fully-operational guest ranch in 1948 and continued to operate for more than seventy strong years. In 2021, the Gant family transferred ownership to a duo of families who were frequent guests of the property as well as admirers of the warm, always-present, Southwestern hospitality.

Since transferring ownership, the families and a new management team have upgraded the facilities to reflect their care and dedication for the ranch while maintaining exceptional levels of service. The traditions of the Spanish *caballeros*, "the gentlemen on horseback," are treasured to this day to ensure that the legacy of Rancho de los Caballeros lasts an eternity.

The kitchens at the ranch are run by newly promoted Executive Chef Robert Cornett. Chef Robert manages the three on-site restaurants, directs all front- and back-of-house kitchen staff, and leads development of the ranch's innovative culinary programming like the Desert Cookouts, Ranch Reserve: Wine Evenings at 19, and the annual Guest Chef Series. He joined Rancho de los Caballeros in 2022 as the executive sous chef. Over the last two years, he has significantly contributed to the operations of the Main Dining Room and the Club Grill. Now managing all dining venues, Cornett aims to enhance their Southwest and Americana cuisine with seasonal vegetable-focused menu improvements and elevated smoker techniques.

Serves 1

2 bone-in pork chops	1. Coat the pork chop with herbs.
1/4 oz herbs, sage, parsley, chive, and rosemary, chopped	2. In a sauté pan, sear roast pork over medium to medium-high heat.
Brussels sprouts, as you like	3. Deep fry the Brussels sprouts until tender and crispy and toss with salt, pepper, and brown butter. Set aside.
1/2 cup quinoa dressing (recipe on another page)	
2 tablespoons apple bourbon sauce (recipe follows)	4. When ready to plate, line the quinoa down the center of plate and place the Brussels sprouts on opposite corners of quinoa.
Micro-fine herbs (chopped fresh parsley, chives, tarragon, and chervil)	5. Slice pork chop between the bones and place on top of the quinoa.
Salt and pepper, to taste	6. Top with apple bourbon and micro-fine herbs.
Brown butter	

Apple Bourbon Sauce
Serves 15

2 tablespoons butter

1/2 cup shallots, minced

2 pounds apple, peeled and sliced

2 tablespoons lemon juice

2 tablespoons apple cider vinegar

6 tablespoons brown sugar

1 tablespoon Worcestershire sauce

1/4 cup chicken stock

1 1/2 cups bourbon

1. In a saucepan, melt butter over medium-high heat.
2. Add the shallots and cook until soft. Add the apples, bring to simmer, and cook for 5 minutes.
3. Add lemon juice, apple cider vinegar, brown sugar, Worcestershire sauce, and chicken stock. Simmer for 20 minutes.
4. Add the bourbon, return to simmer, and cook for 5 more minutes
5. Remove from heat and adjust seasoning as needed.
6. Puree the mixture with a blender until smooth.

★ SMOKED CHICKEN ENCHILADAS

Rancho de los Caballeros, Wickenburg, Arizona

Serves 4

1 gallon water	1. Combine all ingredients except for ice and chicken and bring to boil.
1 cup salt	2. Add ice and chill.
1 cup sugar	3. Add chicken and brine for 24 hours.
4 tablespoons pink peppercorn	4. Once brined, lather chicken generously with chicken marinade (Mojo Rojo) for at least an hour.
1 bunch thyme	
2 oranges, sliced	
2 lemons, sliced	5. Smoke chicken at 225°F for 4 hours or until internal temperature reaches 165°F.
2 limes, sliced	
10 bay leaves	6. Make the chipotle salsa, black bean puree, and cilantro crema and refrigerate until ready to use.
1 gallon ice	
Chicken, whole, around 3 pounds	7. When ready to serve, fill and roll each tortilla with a 1/4-cup of chicken and a tablespoon of cheese.
Mojo Rojo (recipe follows)	
Chipotle salsa (recipe follows)	
Black bean puree (recipe follows)	8. In a small pan, add a 1/4-cup of chipotle salsa and place enchiladas in pan. Top with rest of salsa.
Cilantro crema (recipe follows)	
12 flour tortillas	9. Bake in oven for 10 minutes at 350°F.
Metling cheese, like Oaxacan, jack, or mozzarella	10. Place Bean Puree in middle of plate. With a spoon, spread beans in a circular motion.
	11. Place 3 enchiladas on top and add the cilantro crema over the top.

Chicken Marinade (Mojo Rojo)
Serves 9

24 fresh whole garlic cloves, peeled	1. Place the Morita chilies in hot water for 20 minutes to soften and strain.
6 Morita chilies	
1 1/2 cups water	2. Combine all the ingredients, except the oil, into a blender and puree until smooth.
2 tablespoons paprika	
1 tablespoon salt	3. Emulsify the oil into puree.
1 tablespoon cumin	
1 tablespoon sherry vinegar	
3 cups olive oil	

Black Bean Puree
Serves 3

1 10-ounce can black beans	1. Place the black beans and salsa together in a bowl or blender.
Chipotle salsa (recipe follows)	2. Blend until smooth.

Chipotle Salsa
Serves 10

2 Morita chilies, diced 1 pound tomatoes, diced 1 tablespoon garlic, minced (about 4 cloves) 1/2 yellow onion, peeled & diced Salt, to taste 1 cup diced cilantro	1. Place the Morita chilies in hot water for 20 minutes to soften and then strain. 2. Roast tomatoes, garlic, and onion at 425°F for about 30 minutes or until charred 3. Combine all ingredients and taste to season.

Cilantro Crema
Serves 10

1 cup cilantro, chopped 2 tablespoons lime juice 1 tablespoon garlic, minced (about 4 cloves) 1/2 cup sour cream Salt and pepper, to taste	1. Combine all ingredients together in a bowl or blender. 2. Blend until smooth.

MAIN DISHES & ENTRÉES 53

★ SZECHUAN ZA'ATAR CORNISH HENS

Flat Creek Ranch, Flat Creek, Wyoming

This recipe, which is paired with Orange Bourbon Carrots and Pastina (recipes on other pages), is shared by chef Jake VanRy at Flat Creek Ranch. *See the Pastina recipe for the history of the ranch.*

Serves 8

4 Cornish hens	1. Start by cutting the spine out of your hens with kitchen shears then cut down the breast bone to cut in in half. Salt both sides of each half liberally and place on a sheet tray with drying rack. Rest uncovered in a fridge for a day or at least 6 hours.
Salt, as you like	
2 cups neutral tasting oil	
1/4 cup Za'atar	
2 tablespoons garam masala	
1 tablespoon garlic powder	2. Preheat oven to 400°F. Remove the hens from the fridge and pat the pieces dry with a paper towel. Combine neutral oil with za'atar, garam masala, garlic powder, onion powder, black pepper, and Szechuan oil and mix until thoroughly combined with no remaining lumps. Brush hens with oil and put them in the oven for 45–55 minutes or until internal temperature reaches 165°F.
1 tablespoon onion powder	
2 teaspoons freshly ground black pepper	
2 tablespoons Szechuan oil	
2 purple carrots, for garnish	
1 orange carrot, for garnish	
Pomegranate seeds, for garnish	
6 tablespoons salmon roe, for garnish	3. To plate the hens, carrots, and patina, ladle about 3/4 cup of the pastina into the center of the plate, then place hen vertical in the center of the Pastina. Lean two carrots atop the hens (preferably different colors for appearance). For garnish, place 5–7 pomegranate seeds in a star pattern around the hen with salmon roe in the middle of each. Squeeze 5 drops of butternut puree making each one bigger than the next (see image). Quarter golden berries and place on puree drops, skipping every other one. With a mandolin, slice the remaining carrot to 1/16-inch and place opposing the golden berries.
Butternut puree, for garnish	
8 golden berries, for garnish	

★ SONORAN SPICE BRISKET

White Stallion Ranch, Tucson, Arizona

Chef Judy came up with this recipe, along with many of the others that she still uses on ranch to this day. *See the Breakfast Ride Potatoes recipe for the history of the ranch.*

Serves 10–12

- 6–7-pound brisket
- 1/2 cup garlic powder
- 1/4 cup dried coriander
- 1/2 cup chili powder
- 2 tablespoons ground cumin
- 1/2 cup paprika
- 1/2 cup dried oregano
- 1 teaspoon pepper
- 1/2 cup salt
- 4–5 cups water

1. Combine all the ingredients, except brisket, in a bowl and blend well.
2. Rub mixture all over meat before grilling. Place the meat in a pan and add the water.
3. Bake 4–6 hours, depending on size, at 250°F in a convection oven or 350°F in a regular oven.
4. When tender, remove the meat from the pan and allow to sit, covered with foil, for about 20 minutes so the juices will be absorbed back into the meat.
5. Slice and serve.

★ PRICKLY PEAR MARGARITA ★

White Stallion Ranch, Tucson, Arizona

Prickly pear cactuses grow wild all over southern Arizona, and people have been using their fruits and leaves for generations to create recipes. This recipe was created by Michael True.

Makes 1 drink

- 2 ounces margarita mix
- 2 ounces tequila
- 1/4 ounce triple Sec
- 3/4 ounce prickly pear syrup
- 1 ounce 7-Up

1. Combine all the ingredients and stir to blend.
2. Serve over crushed ice in a salted-rim glass.

★ BOSS MAN COCKTAIL ★

Kara Creek Ranch, Sundance, Wyoming

The Kara Creek Saloon was established in 2017 alongside the Snook Mercantile. This gives guests an old West saloon vibe and a place for them to relax with live Western music and a cold beer or a glass of whiskey after a long day of working cattle. This is one of the saloon's most popular drinks. It's their special twist on a Moscow mule and is served by their friendly bartender.

Makes 1 drink

2 ounces Pendleton whiskey 2 ounces ginger beer 2 ounces ginger ale 1 fresh squeezed lime Ice	1. Fill a Moscow Mule mug (or highball glass) with ice, then add the whiskey and lime juice. 2. Top with the beer and soda.

★ TATER TOT CASSEROLE

Kara Creek Ranch, Sundance, Wyoming

Kara Creek Ranch was founded in 2000, but their roots trace back to the early 1800s with the pioneering spirit of their great-great-grandfather. He courageously trailed cattle from the expansive plains of Texas to this rugged terrain. Over generations, they cultivated a deep connection to the land, nurturing both its resources and cherished traditions. Today, the family remains steadfast in their commitment to preserving its heritage while embracing modern practices to ensure its sustainability for future generations.

With over 5,000 cattle grazing freely across 70,000 acres of mountains, fields, hills, and prairies, Kara Creek Ranch primarily raises Black and Red Angus, taking pride in their care and well-being. The food at the ranch is typical cowboy-style food featuring mainly home-raised beef, potatoes, pasta, and vegetables. They serve a large American style breakfast including, but not limited to, bacon, eggs, toast, pancakes, pastries, and fruit. Each day is rounded out with a large dinner served family-style. This dish is a guest favorite.

Serves 8

1 pound ground beef	1. Sauté the ground beef, onion, and salt and pepper in a frying pan over medium heat.
1 onion, peeled and diced	2. Place the beef mixture into a greased 9 x 13-inch baking dish.
Salt and pepper, to taste	3. Spoon the soup over the beef and top with the green beans.
1 10.5-ounce can cream of mushroom soup	4. Place the tater tots uniformly on top of the mixture and bake in a 350°F oven for about 40 minutes or until all tater tots are crispy and the mixture is bubbling through.
Milk, enough to thin the soup to a thick consistency	
1 14.5-ounce can green beans	
2 cups tater tots, frozen	

★ CHICKEN FRIED STEAK

Kara Creek Ranch, Sundance, Wyoming

This is a favorite at the ranch and is typically paired with mashed potatoes, gravy, and a vegetable chosen by the cook each day. It's also made with home-raised tenderized cube steak.

Serves 4

- 4 cube steaks
- 4 eggs
- 1/4 cup milk
- Salt and pepper, to taste
- 1 teaspoon garlic powder
- 1 teaspoon onion powder
- 1 cup all-purpose flour
- 1 cup breadcrumbs
- 1/2 cup crushed saltine crackers
- 1/4 cup parmesan cheese
- 1 1/2 cups oil, for frying
- Gravy (recipe follows)

1. Combine the eggs, milk, salt, pepper, and garlic and onion powders together in a shallow bowl. Whisk together. Set aside.
2. In another shallow dish, combine the remaining ingredients, except the oil.
3. Dip the meat into the egg mixture and then into the flour mixture. Do this until the steaks are coated.
4. Heat the oil in a sauté pan over medium high heat and gently add the steaks. Cook the steak on one side until it's golden for about 3–4 minutes and then flip over and cook an additional 2–3 minutes. Remove and drain on paper towels.

Gravy
Makes 2 Cups

- 1/4 cup leftover frying oil
- 1/4 cup leftover flour dredge
- 2 cups whole milk
- 1/2 teaspoon salt
- 1/2 teaspoon freshly ground black pepper

1. Stir the flour mixture into the oil and whisk continuously until golden brown, or about 3 minutes. Add the milk and whisk to combine.
2. Bring to a simmer and cook, stirring occasionally until thickened, 5–6 minutes. Season with salt and pepper.

MAIN DISHES & ENTRÉES 61

★ HUCKLEBERRY GLAZED MEATLOAF

Circle Bar Ranch, Utica, Montana

The Circle Bar Ranch was originally inhabited by the Blackfeet Native Americans who used it as a hunting ground. By the late 1800s, the United States of America claimed primary ownership of the area, and men began staking out their claim on the land. The ranch assumed the name "S Lazy 4 Bar" in 1890, which was one of the earliest brands in Montana.

The land later became the Middle Fork Cattle Company and was used to buy, sell, and raise cattle and horses. The business eventually developed into a hunting and recreation business, and in 1904, the owners procured a hotel license, as they planned to serve meals and become a guest facility. In 1920, the ranch took on the new brand and name of Circle Bar Ranch.

Huckleberries are native to the Northwestern U.S. and have become a signature ingredient in Montana, found in a variety of products from huckleberry jam to ice cream. The Circle Bar Guest Ranch enjoys highlighting the berries, which are in season during summer months, in its meals and recipes to offer its guests a special taste of Montana.

Serves 6–8

2 teaspoons butter or oil	1. Preheat oven to 350°F.
1 large onion, chopped	2. Melt the butter in a sauce pan and add pepper and onion and cook over medium heat for about 7 minutes or until soft. Let cool slightly.
1 large green bell pepper, chopped	
2 to 2 1/2 pounds ground beef	
1 cup ketchup	3. Place the remaining ingredients in a mixing bowl, then add the pepper and onion and mix together thoroughly.
1 tablespoon Worcestershire sauce	
2 eggs	
1 teaspoon salt	4. Place in greased loaf pan or in a loaf shape on a parchment lined sheet pan.
3/4 teaspoon pepper	
1 cup oatmeal	5. Pour half of the huckleberry glaze on top of meatloaf and bake for 1 hour.
3/4 cup crushed saltine crackers	6. Let rest for 15 minutes.
3/4 cup water	7. Serve with additional glaze on slices of meatloaf with your favorite side dish, such as
Huckleberry glaze (recipe follows)	

Huckleberry Glaze
Makes 2 Cups

- 3 cups fresh or frozen huckleberries
- 4 cups ketchup
- 1/2 cup brown sugar
- 1/3 cup white wine vinegar
- 1 teaspoon Liquid smoke
- 1 tablespoon Worcestershire sauce
- 1/4 cup hot coffee
- 1 teaspoon black pepper
- 2 dashes ghost pepper sauce

Combine all sauce ingredients in sauce pan and simmer for 10 minutes.

★ BLACK ANGUS RIB-EYE COWBOY STEAK

The Broadmoor's Ranch at Emerald Valley, Colorado Springs, Colorado

In 1904, the Grace Episcopal Church built the original cabin at Camp Vigil (ve-heel) for a recreation center and built a church retreat camp on land they leased from the Forest Service. In 1920, a donation will allowed Girl Scouts to purchase Camp Vigil in 1921. In 1923, Spencer Penrose created the "Mountain Trails Association" and bought Camp Vigil from the Girl Scouts. The land was used for private cabins for himself and his friends, Claude Boettcher, Carl Pforzheimer, and Henry Blackmer, in the form of a subscription membership club. Between 1923 and 1924 they added electricity, phones, water, and a septic system.

In January 1924, Swiss Chalet cabins and a clubhouse were built. "A clubhouse to cost $10,000 is being built of native logs with large fireplaces, and the Old Camp Vigil cabin, formerly the Girl Scout headquarters for summer camp, will be used in the colony plan." In June 1926, Jack Dempsey arrived to train at Camp Vigil for a month. Prior to that, he was a roustabout and miner in Cripple Creek from 1911 to 1916, where he began boxing under the name of "Kid Blackie." Later, he became known as the "Manassa Mauler" after winning the heavyweight title for the first time in 1919. In the summer of 1939, Spencer Penrose had his two cabins removed and placed them at Rosemont Reservoir and combined them to make a fishing lodge. Sadly, he died that year. Three years later Camp Vigil was donated to the community as "Camp Vigil, Inc. for the use of non-profits, i.e., Boys Club, Girl Scouts, Boy Scouts, etc."

It was 1946 when Don Danvers of San Antonio purchased the property to turn it into a dude ranch. He renamed it Emerald Valley Ranch. In 1982, Mike and Katie Turley acquired the ranch and opened it for weddings and corporate retreats. Then, in 2012, the Broadmoor Hotel bought The Ranch at Emerald Valley and obtained a particular use permit from the U.S. Forest Service. They briefly opened in 2013 but were washed out by rains. They opened the next year for a full season and have been open since.

See the Bacon & Brown Butter Cast-Iron Trout recipe for the history of the Broadmoor.

Serves 1–2

32-ounce rib-eye steak	1. Rub the steak with oil, then heavily season with salt and pepper.
olive oil, as needed	
salt, as needed	2. Place the steak on a hot grill and cook 6–8 minutes per side for medium-rare or longer if a less rare steak is desired.
pepper, as needed	
Horseradish black pepper cream (recipe follows)	3. Remove from grill and let rest 8–10 minutes before slicing. Serve with horseradish black pepper cream.

Horseradish Black Pepper Cream
Makes about 1 1/2 cups

1 cup sour cream
1/4 cup horseradish
1/2 teaspoon salt
1/2 teaspoon black pepper
1/8 teaspoon Worcestershire sauce
1/8 teaspoon tabasco sauce

1. Combine all ingredients in a bowl using a whisk or a spoon.
2. Store in a container inside the refrigerator.

★ BUFFALOAF
Medicine Bow Lodge, Saratoga, Wyoming

Tim and Debbie Bishop bought Medicine Bow Lodge and Adventure Guest Ranch in 2002, fulfilling a dream they formed while working and meeting at a guest ranch during their college years. It was a process to find a ranch that met their desires for their family. After searching for five years, they found Medicine Bow Lodge. They made the move with their 13-year-old, 12-year-old, and 10-year-old children. It was an exciting time and an adventure for a Southern family from Louisiana. The children were involved in the family business until they graduated but have since built their own lives with growing families.

The ranch is rich in history. The Lodge was built in 1917 with the original kitchen and dining room still intact where guests enjoy delicious meals. The ranch is located in the unique mountains of Wyoming and in the Medicine Bow National Forest. It's nestled up against Barrett Ridge that overlooks Barrett Creek. After a day of ranch activities, guests can enjoy a scrumptious supper prepared by Chef Debbie and then gather around an evening campfire with smores fixings. Tim and Debbie are hands on and interact with their guests from the time they arrive until they leave. The Bishops mean it when they say, "Keeping it real and authentic." It's the theme that is carried throughout the ranch and includes Chef Debbie's cuisine.

Guest have described her cooking as being elegant, rustic gourmet dining. Chef Debbie's talent takes her to building and blending succulent flavors while using only the finest ingredients. She contributes her love for cooking to her Mamma Lanier, who allowed her to cook with her and taught her how to make everything from scratch. She has kept up with staying true to cooking homemade from salad dressings, sauces, breads, unique salads, soups, entrees, and desserts. Tim and Chef Debbie share duties in the kitchen, with Tim overseeing breakfast, including cinnamon rolls. The recipe shared in this book are guest favorites.

Chef Debbie shared, "It was hard to choose, but these were some of the most requested on the menu. Since Tim and I have been at Medicine Bow Lodge, I have enjoyed cooking with buffalo. I love the taste of bison and knowing it is a lean meat. A favorite of our guests is my Buffaloaf. I have taken my Mamma's recipe and tweaked it using bison with some other changes. The herbs are key in this dish, and the topping will make you want more. The fresh ginger is a distinguished taste that adds so much flavor. I pair Buffaloaf with savory sweet potatoes and steamed broccoli or green beans almondine. Enjoy!"

Makes 2 bread loaf pans

4 pounds ground Bison	1. Preheat oven to 375°F.
1 bell pepper, chopped	2. Place all ingredients in a large bowl. Use your hands and mix well to combine all ingredients. Put the meat mixture in a prepared loaf pan. Place half of the glaze on top of the Buffaloaf.
1 white onion, chopped	
1 red onion, chopped	
2 teaspoons Worcestershire sauce	
1 1/2 teaspoons each of dried thyme, dried oregano, and rosemary	3. Cover with foil and bake for 1 1/2 hours. It will be done when internal temperature reaches 160°F. Sometimes it can take up to 2 hours. Uncover and add remainder of glaze and place back in oven for 15 minutes until it bubbles. Remove from oven and let rest for 10–15 minutes.
1 1/2 heaping teaspoons fine Himalayan salt	
1 teaspoon crushed black pepper (maybe a little more)	
1 14.5-ounce can chopped tomatoes, drained well	
1 6-ounce can tomato paste	
3/4 cup of oatmeal, ground in blender	
2 eggs, well beaten	
Glaze topping (recipe follows)	

Buffaloaf Glaze
Makes about 2 1/2 cups

2 cups of ketchup	Combine in a bowl and stir until blended.
1/4 cup Worcestershire sauce	
2 heaping teaspoons fresh ginger	
1/3 cup dried mustard	
1/2 cup of brown sugar	

★ BISON SHORT RIBS

Lone Mountain Ranch, Big Sky, Montana

Horn and Cantle at Lone Mountain Ranch embodies traditional cooking techniques in their braised short rib dish and is a testament to the enduring practices of ranch cuisine. Braising, an essential method in ranch cooking, allows for rich, tender flavors to develop as the dish is slowly cooked in a Dutch oven over an open fire. This time-honored approach not only enhances the short ribs' succulence but also connects diners to the rustic, open-air culinary heritage ranch cuisine. *See the Cedar Plank Mushrooms recipe for the history of the ranch.*

Serves 6

6 portion bison short ribs

Salt and fresh cracked pepper

Flour, for dredging

2 tablespoons oil

2 quarts mirepoix (equal parts carrot, celery and onion), chopped

15 fresh whole garlic cloves, peeled

1 quart San Marzano tomatoes, pureed

1 quart red wine

2 quarts demi-glace or brown stock

1/4 cup each fresh rosemary and thyme

1. Season the short rib portions with salt and fresh cracked pepper and dredge with flour (skip the flour for GF).

2. Heat the oil over medium high heat in the braising pan you will cook them in and sear the short ribs. Remove the short ribs and set aside.

3. Add the mirepoix and garlic and cook the mixture for about 7 minutes or until the onions are translucent. Deglaze with red wine and reduce the wine by half. Add the tomato puree and reduce by half.

4. Add the short ribs back into the pan, add demi-glace, rosemary, and thyme (the short ribs should be 3/4 covered by the braising liquid). Bring the liquid to a low boil, remove from heat cover, and cook at 250°F for 5 1/2–6 hours. Rotate the short ribs about halfway through the cooking process to ensure even cooking. For the best results, let the short ribs cool overnight in the braising liquid.

5. When ready to serve, reheat short ribs in oven at 300° degrees for about 15 minutes or until they are heated through. Remove short ribs from braising liquid, bring the liquid to a boil, and then strain through a fine mesh strainer. The liquid may need to be thickened with a roux or cornstarch slurry. The short ribs and gravy are now ready to be served. Serve with Jalapeno Cheddar Polenta and roasted root vegetables (recipes in Side Dishes).

CHAPTER FIVE

DESSERTS & SNACKS

★ WHITE CHOCOLATE CHIP COOKIES

White Stallion Ranch, Tucson, Arizona

These cookies have been served at the ranch since the Trues took over and hired Chef Judy Bellini. She was the first employee hired by Allen True when he bought the ranch in 1965. She was seventeen years old and is still serving up dishes at the ranch today! Third-generation Steven True said, "She babysat my father, my uncle, and me and my brother too! She married here, and her husband was also an employee until he retired (he has since passed), and her kids were raised here." *See the Breakfast Ride Potatoes recipe for the history of the ranch.*

Makes 24

- 1 cup shortening
- 1 cup white sugar
- 1 cup brown sugar
- 2 eggs
- 1 teaspoon vanilla
- 2 cups coarsely crushed potato chips
- 1 6-ounce package white chocolate chips
- 2 1/2 cups flour
- 1 teaspoon baking soda

1. Cream shortening and sugars together in a large bowl until light in color.
2. Add the eggs and vanilla and beat well.
3. Add the crushed potato chips and white chocolate chips and stir to blend.
4. Sift flour and baking soda in a small bowl and stir into creamed mixture.
5. Drop by tablespoon on a greased cookie sheet and bake at 375°F for 10–12 minutes.

★ HUCKLEBERRY LEMON CRUMB COOKIES

Circle Bar Guest Ranch, Utica, Montana

See the Huckleberry Glazed Meatloaf recipe for the history of the ranch.

Makes 12 large

2 sticks butter, softened	1. Preheat oven to 375°F.
1 cup brown sugar	2. Cream butter and sugars together until smooth. Add lemon zest, lemon juice, eggs, sour cream, and lavender and mix until combined.
1 1/3 cup white sugar	
1 tablespoon lemon zest	
2 teaspoons lemon juice	3. Add flour, baking powder, 4 tablespoons graham crackers crumbs, and salt. Stir until just combined, then fold in huckleberries.
2 eggs, room temperature	
1/2 cup sour cream	
1/2 teaspoon ground lavender	4. Scoop out 24 balls using a large cookie scoop and roll them in remaining graham cracker crumbs.
4 cups all-purpose flour	
3 teaspoons baking powder	
4 tablespoons graham cracker crumbs	5. Place on parchment lined cookie sheet and bake for 12–14 minutes.
1/2 teaspoon salt	
2 cups huckleberries	6. When done, cool on cooling rack. Drizzle glaze across the cookies.
1/2 cup graham cracker crumbs (for rolling cookie balls)	
Lemon glaze (recipe follows)	

Lemon Glaze
Makes about 1 cup

1 cup powdered sugar	Combine glaze ingredients in a bowl and whisk together. Add more lemon juice if needed to make a glaze.
1 teaspoon lemon zest	
4 teaspoons lemon juice	

★ TIM'S ICED OATMEAL COOKIES

Medicine Bow Lodge, Saratoga, Wyoming

These cookies ARE the most requested to fill the ranch's cookie jar and the most popular recipe ask. Guests have been known to join Tim and Debbie in the kitchen to learn how to make these delicious cookies. Baggies are always on hand for guests who want some for the trip home. Debbie notes, "The key is the consistency with the oatmeal to form the cookie dough."

Makes 2 1/2 dozen

- 1 1/2 cups all-purpose flour
- 1 tablespoon baking powder
- 1 teaspoon baking soda
- 1 tablespoon cinnamon
- 3/4 cup packed brown sugar
- 1/2 cup white sugar
- 1 teaspoon vanilla
- 1 tablespoon molasses
- 2 large eggs
- 1 1/2 sticks butter, melted
- 3–4 cups oats

1. Combine the first 4 ingredients together in a bowl and blend. Then add next 4 ingredients and stir to combine.
2. Stir in the eggs and mix well. Next, add the butter and mix well. Finally, add the oats and blend well, but do not overbeat.
3. Roll dough in hand to make medium-sized balls. Place on cookie sheet and bake for 10–12 minutes. Do not overcook, or they will be hard. Place on a wire cooking rack and let cool. Drizzle powdered sugar icing (recipe follows) on top as little or as much as preferred onto cooled cookies.

Almond Icing
Makes about 1/2 cup

- 1 cup powdered sugar
- 1/2 teaspoon almond extract
- Water

Whisk ingredients in a bowl being careful not to add too much water. The consistency should be thick enough to drizzle over the cookie.

★ CARROT COOKIES

Sylvan Dale Ranch, Loveland, Colorado

A Loveland, Colorado, couple recalled this of Tillie and her cooking. "When we think of Tillie's kitchen, we think of warm conversations around the table with food, friends, and her beautiful smile that still glows like it did years ago." *See Tillie's Cinnamon Rolls for the history of the ranch.*

Makes 2 dozen

2 eggs, beaten 2/3 cup neutral oil 2/3 cup white sugar 1/4 teaspoon vanilla 2/3 cup carrots, cooked and mashed 2 teaspoons orange rind, grated 1 1/2 cups all-purpose flour 1 1/3 teaspoons baking powder 1/2 teaspoon salt Powdered sugar icing *(see facing page)*	1. Mix the first 4 ingredients in a large bowl and stir. Add the carrots and orange rind and stir to blend. 2. Sift dry ingredients together in a small bowl and gradually stir into the wet ingredients. 3. Drop by teaspoonful onto a greased cookie sheet and bake at 350°F for 15 minutes or until slightly brown. 4. Cool and frost with powdered sugar icing.

★ ANGEL THUMBPRINT COOKIES

Sylvan Dale Ranch, Loveland, Colorado

This ranch has been family owned and operated since 1946. The story of this recipe is from one of their granddaughters called "Little Liska." She recalled, "There is such a thing as heaven on Earth! I experienced it every time I came through my grandmother's back door. Each and every day of my young life I was blessed with the aroma of 'love' and gracefully shown the beauty of hard work. This was mixed with a delicious blend of artistic ability that shaped each roll, every loaf, and created those sweet treats that were unforgettable to the senses and beyond. But out of all the tastes of this and bites of that, none are as heavenly as my grandma's Grand's Angel Thumbprint cookies. Perhaps it is the egg white that coats the outside with a delightful amber color and makes the bottom crispy, or maybe it is the homemade apple jelly that sits like a polished jewel in the center with chopped walnuts hugging its edges. But there is one thing I am quite sure of… the only angel I have ever seen putting thumb prints in those cookies was Noni!" *See Tillie's Cinnamon Rolls for the history of the ranch.*

Makes 8 dozen

4 sticks butter, room temperature	1. Combine butter and sugar in a large mixing bowl and cream until fluffy.
2 cups brown sugar	2. Add the egg yolks, vanilla, and almond extract and beat well. Stir in the baking powder and flour and stir to combine.
4 eggs, separated	3. Shape the dough into 3/4-inch balls. Dip in egg whites and roll in walnuts.
4 teaspoons vanilla	4. Place on a buttered or lined cookie sheet and press down the center with the thumb and fill with homemade jelly.
1 teaspoon almond extract	5. Bake at 350°F for about 15 minutes or until lightly browned.
1 teaspoon baking powder	
4 cups all-purpose flour	
2 cups walnuts, finely chopped	
Jelly for filling	

★ COWBOY COOKIES

Drowsy Water Ranch, Granby, Colorado

These cookies are made each week at the ranch and are packed in the saddlebags for the riders. They enjoy the huge cookies while eating lunch on the trail and look forward to returning to the ranch for their famous cookies year after year. Many of the ranch's recipes came with the ranch and have been made on a weekly basis for years! *See the High-Altitude Cornbread recipe for the history of the ranch.*

Makes 20 (BIG!) cookies

- 2 sticks butter or margarine
- 1 cup packed brown sugar
- 1 cup white sugar
- 2 large eggs
- 1 teaspoon vanilla
- 2 cups all-purpose flour
- 1 teaspoon baking soda
- 2 teaspoons baking powder
- 1/2 teaspoon salt
- 2 cups old-fashioned oats
- 3/4 cup chocolate chips
- 1/2 cup nuts, chopped

1. Cream together the butter, sugars, and eggs until light and fluffy, stirring frequently. Add the vanilla.
2. In a separate bowl, stir together flour, soda, baking powder, salt, and oats.
3. Fold the dry ingredients into the butter/sugar mixture and stir. The dough should be stiff but if too soft, add more flour.
4. Stir in the chocolate chips and nuts.
5. Preheat the oven to 350°F.
6. Roll the dough into 1/4-cup balls and place on a cookie sheet lined with parchment paper or lightly greased, leaving about 3 inches between cookies to allow them to spread.
7. Bake for 10–15 minutes, rotating sheet halfway through. They should be golden but still spongy when done for a chewy texture.
8. Leave on the cookie sheet to cool until set. The cooking time should be reduced if smaller cookies are desired.

★ BLUEBERRY PIE

Medicine Bow Lodge, Saratoga, Wyoming

This recipe was shared by Medicine Bow's Chef Debbie. She wrote, "I am privileged to have inherited my Mamma's recipe books, which included her personal recipes. One day, I was going through a pie recipe book and a piece of paper fell out that was in her handwriting. It was the Blueberry Pie recipe. At the top of the paper it read, 'This pie is out of the world!' I knew that I had to try it. I have adjusted it some because her recipe was loaded with sugar! That's a grandma for you. This pie has amazing flavor with me adding pure almond extract to the blueberries. I have had whole pies disappear from the dessert table and the pie pan return to the kitchen empty. I am filled with joy when this happens." *See the Buffaloaf recipe for more the history of the lodge.*

Makes 1 pie

1 deep dish unbaked pie crust
3 cups frozen or fresh blueberries
1 1/2 teaspoons pure almond extract
1 1/2 teaspoons sugar
1 cup sugar
1/3 cup all-purpose flour
Dash salt
2 eggs, beaten well
1/2 cup sour cream

Crumble topping (makes about 1 cup)
1/2 cup sugar
1/2 cup all-purpose flour
4 tablespoons cold butter

1. Place the blueberries, 1 1/2 teaspoons sugar, and almond extract into a bowl. Mix gently to incorporate flavors with the berries. Set aside.
2. Combine the next 5 ingredients in a bowl and stir until you have a creamy consistency. Set aside.
3. To make the crumble topping, combine the sugar, flour, and butter in a food processor or mix with a fork. It should be the consistency of cornmeal.
4. Place the macerated blueberries in the bottom of the pie crust. Pour the creamy mixture evenly over the berries. Sprinkle crumble on top of the pie.
5. Place in 350°F oven for 50–60 minutes. (A pie crust guard or foil may be needed for the last 20 minutes so the crust won't burn.) The pie needs to be set, without much jiggle. Remove from the oven. Let it cool for at least 45 minutes. Serve with vanilla bean ice cream.

★ RHUBARB PIE

Latigo Ranch, Kremmling, Colorado

From Lisa at the ranch. "The gardening season at our elevation is very short except for hardy plants like rhubarb. We harvest enough rhubarb for two pies each week from our opening in early June through mid to late September. It is served at the Friday night cookout along with peanut butter pie and maybe an apple or blueberry pie. This rhubarb pie is a delicious farm-to-table dessert." *See the Caramel Popcorn recipe for the history of the ranch.*

Makes 1 pie

- 2 cups rhubarb, fresh or frozen (don't drain if frozen), chopped
- 1 cup white sugar
- 1 tablespoon flour
- 1 egg
- 2 cups all-purpose flour
- 1/2 cup neutral oil
- 1/4 cup milk
- 1 tablespoon lemon juice

1. Combine fresh rhubarb, sugar, tablespoon of flour, and egg together in a bowl and set aside. If the rhubarb is frozen, microwave the rhubarb and sugar together until warm but not hot and then stir in the flour and the egg.

2. Combine the flour, oil, milk, and lemon juice together in a bowl and mix by hand. Divide dough in half. Shape into equal balls and chill for about 30 minutes.

3. Roll out one ball between sheets of parchment. Carefully release the top sheet and place back on the rolled-out dough to loosen it. Turn it over and release the dough from this side to loosen it. Turn an empty 9-inch pie plate upside down and place on top of the dough, slide a hand underneath, and carefully turn over onto the counter. Release the parchment and gently work the dough into the pie plate so that there aren't any air pockets.

4. Pour the filling into the pie pan. Roll the next dough ball out between the two sheets of parchment. Release the parchment as in the previous step. Slide a hand underneath the bottom parchment and line it up so that it will cover the top of the pie accurately and gently lay it down. Trim off the excess crust, pinch the edges together, poke steam slits decoratively on the top layer, and bake in a 350°F oven for about 50 minutes. Place a lined baking sheet pan under in case it bubbles over. Cool before slicing.

DESSERTS & SNACKS 81

★ BRULÉE WITH HUCKLEBERRIES

Red Rock Ranch, Kelly, Wyoming

This dessert is served at the ranch's Thursday Gourmet dinner *See the Green Chili Grits recipe for the history of the ranch.*

Makes 4

- 2 cups cream
- 1/4 cup white sugar
- 3 eggs, room temperature
- 1 teaspoon vanilla extract
- Fresh huckleberries
- Sugar for topping

1. Place the cream and sugar in a saucepan and warm over low heat to scald (just until bubbles form on the outside). Remove from heat.
2. Beat the eggs and slowly, while constantly whisking, add them to the cream and sugar until incorporated. Cool 8 hours.
3. Fill Brulée cups with mixture and add 1/2 tablespoon of huckleberries in center of cups.
4. Place in a pan and add enough water to come half-way up the Brulée cups. Bake covered at 325°F for 25–35 minutes or until set with a slight jiggle in the center.
5. Chill 4 hours.
6. Spoon 1 tablespoon sugar over each cup.
7. Caramelize with a torch and serve.

★ MAUREEN'S UNDONE BROWNIES

Flathead Lake Lodge, Bigfork, Montana

The original recipe for these brownies came from a lady named Ellette, who Maureen cooked with in 1977. Maureen didn't like the traditional cake brownies that so many people served, so she found a recipe that was fudgy, did some minor tweaking, and topped it with powdered sugar. From the ranch: "Advice—be sure to add the salt to the brownies! If you've been a guest of the lodge, you've likely dug into one of these chocolate delights during your stay, as they are a staple during our Wednesday night steak fry. From us to you, we hope you enjoy this 'sweet' gift." *See the Cheddar Bread recipe for the history of the ranch.*

Make 20, 3-inch squares

- 2 sticks butter, melted
- 1/4 pound unsweetened chocolate
- 2 cups sugar
- 4 eggs
- 1 1/3 cups all-purpose flour
- 2 teaspoons vanilla

1. Preheat oven to 350° degrees. Grease desired baking dish (a large sheet pan or two is recommended).
2. Melt chocolate and butter in a saucepan over low heat. Remove from heat and add the eggs, sugar, and vanilla. Gradually whisk in the flour.
3. Pour into greased baking dish and bake for about 20 minutes or until the sides begin to pull away from the edges of the pan.
4. Allow the brownies to rest for 15 minutes. Cut, serve, and enjoy!

★ MAHOGANY CAKE

Sylvan Dale Ranch, Loveland, Colorado

Pat Spratt from Sand Springs, Oklahoma, recalled her visits to Sylvan Dale Ranch. "I remember so many wonderful times—Mayme's rolls and pies and birthday cake she would bake for us. I'm so proud to have a cabin named for Dinty. The magic of Sylvan Dale lives in my family. From my parents to my grandchildren, they all love it. I hope someday my great-grandchildren will be able to have some wonderful memories of the ranch." *See Tillie's Cinnamon Rolls for the history of the ranch.*

Makes 1 cake

- 1 cup milk
- 1 tablespoon vinegar
- 2 sticks butter or margarine
- 2 cups sugar
- 2 eggs
- 1/2 cup cocoa powder
- 2 1/2 cups all-purpose flour
- 2 teaspoons baking soda
- 1/2 teaspoon salt
- 1 cup hot water
- 1 teaspoon vanilla

1. Mix the milk and vinegar together and set aside. In a separate bowl, cream the butter, sugar, eggs, and cocoa together until well blended. Add the milk/vinegar mixture and stir.
2. Add the flour, baking soda, and salt to the mixture and stir to blend. Add hot water and vanilla and mix thoroughly.
3. Bake in a greased 8 x 11-inch pan at 350°F for 45 minutes or until a toothpick comes out clean.

★ "THE CHUCK" ★

An 1865 Texas cowhand, Albert Erwin, recalled, "Our chuck was composed of beans, meat, sourdough and corn bread and a few canned vegetables. We made and drank black coffee by the gallons. When we had canned vegetables, we broke the chuck monotony with son-of-a-gun stew. Also, during the spring, when we castrated the male yearlings, the chuck monotony would be broken with messes of mountain oysters."

★ Cowboy Coffee

★ Sourdough Bread

★ Bacon

★ Beans & Cornbread

★ Son-of-Gun Stew

★ Splatter Dabs (Hotcakes)

★ Rocky Mountain Oysters

★ NORWEGIAN CREAM CAKE
White Stallion Ranch, Tucson, Arizona

Kristen True shared her story with us about the ranch and this recipe. "I visited White Stallion Ranch for the first time in 1987 with my father and was so lucky to be able to help out in the corrals with the wranglers. This is where I met Michael True for the first time, and after a few years of long-distance dating, we got married at White Stallion Ranch in 1991.

"I grew up in Oslo, Norway, where my passions were any form of skiing, horses, and later in my teenage years, cooking. I completed two years in a culinary school and then went on to do two and a half years of an apprenticeship at a large hotel in Oslo and then a couple of years cooking for a very famous large restaurant in Oslo. This all helped me fit in at White Stallion and to be able to help out in all parts of the ranch.

"I have been running the kitchen for almost twenty years at White Stallion and have incorporated a few Norwegian food dishes, such as Kvæfjordkake (Kvaefjord) Cake or what most Norwegians refer to simply as 'world's best cake.' It's a light sponge cake with a meringue, sprinkled with sliced almonds. Two layers of cake with a creamy custard and whipped cream filling served with some fresh berries on the side. It has become the favorite dessert at White Stallion, and our guests are always asking if it will be on our menu during their stay here." *See the Breakfast Ride Potatoes recipe for the history of the ranch.*

Makes 1 cake

- 5 1/2 sticks butter
- 3 cups sugar
- 24 egg yolks
- 4 teaspoons vanilla sugar
- 1 1/2 cups milk
- 4 cups flour
- 6 teaspoons baking powder
- 24 egg whites

Filling
- 4 cups sugar
- 1/2 cup sliced almonds
- 1 cup heavy cream
- 1 package instant vanilla pudding mix
- Fresh fruit for garnish

1. Whisk the sugar and butter until smooth and pale. Fold in the egg yolks, vanilla sugar, milk, flour, and baking powder. Mix well.
2. Spread on a 14 x 17-inch baking pan lined with parchment paper.
3. Whisk sugar and egg whites together until stiff peaks to form a meringue. Spread evenly over the base made in step one.
4. Sprinkle almonds on top of the meringue.
5. Bake at 350°F in the lower part of the oven for 25-30 minutes.
6. To make filling, whip the cream and make the vanilla pudding separately. Then mix the cream and vanilla pudding gently together and refrigerate until cold and firm.
7. Let the cake cool after removing it from the oven. Cut it in half.
8. Spread the filling on top of one half and cover the other half.
9. Garnish with fruit or berries.

★ STRAWBERRY SHORTCAKE

The Broadmoor's Ranch at Emerald Valley, Colorado Springs, Colorado

See the Bacon & Brown Butter Cast-Iron Trout recipe for the history of the Broadmoor. Also see the Black Angus Cowboy Ribeye Steak recipe for the history of Emerald Valley Ranch.

Serves 8–10

2 cups flour

2 tablespoons sugar

1/2 teaspoon salt

1/2 teaspoon vanilla extract

1 cup buttermilk, cold

1 stick butter, melted

Macerated Strawberries

1 pint strawberries washed, quartered

2 tablespoons sugar

1/2 each lime zest & juice

Whipped Cream

1 cup heavy cream

3 tablespoons sugar

1 teaspoon vanilla extract

1. Preheat oven to 400°F. Mix flour, sugar, and salt in a medium bowl.
2. In a separate bowl, mix vanilla into buttermilk. Whisk melted butter into cold buttermilk. The buttermilk will solidify into small bits.
3. Stir buttermilk-butter mixture into flour mixture until flour is just moistened. The batter will be lumpy. Portion with a cookie-dough scoop onto parchment-lined sheet trays. Refrigerate for 15 minutes.
4. Bake 10–11 minutes or until golden brown on top and edges. Cool 20 minutes, split, and fill with macerated strawberries and whipped cream. Top with more berries and whipped cream if desired.

Macerated Strawberries: Mix strawberries, sugar, lime juice, and lime zest together. Cover and refrigerate until needed.

Whipped Cream: Combine heavy cream, sugar, and vanilla extract in the bowl of a stand mixer with a whisk attachment. Whip to medium peaks. Refrigerate until needed.

★ BEE'S KNEES COCKTAIL ★

The Broadmoor's Ranch at Emerald Valley, Colorado Springs, Colorado

The Bee's Knees is a classic Prohibition-era cocktail made with gin, honey syrup, and fresh lemon juice. Its name comes from 1920s slang for "the best," and the potent honey and lemon combination was originally used to mask the flavor of low-quality "bathtub" gin. Today, with higher quality spirits available, the drink is celebrated for its balanced, simple, and refreshing sweet-and-sour flavor profile.

Makes 1 drink

- 2 ounces gin, your favorite
- 1 ounce lemon juice
- 1 ounce honey simple syrup
- lemon twist, garnish

1. To make honey simple syrup, dissolve 2 parts honey to 1 part water over slight heat and allow to cool.
2. Combine gin, lemon juice, honey simple syrup, and ice in a pint glass or a shaker. Shake vigorously, strain into a martini glass, and garnish with a lemon twist.

★ CARAMEL CORN
Latigo Ranch, Kremmling, Colorado

Latigo Ranch is located at 9,000 feet above sea level in the heart of the Colorado Rocky Mountains and has been owned by the George family since 1987. They operate as a guest ranch in the summer months and as a Nordic Ski destination vacation spot in the winter. It's a family business with Randy and Lisa at the helm, Spencer as head chef, Amanda as sommelier, and Hannah as head wrangler. It was homesteaded in 1927 by Frank Kasdorf and began as the Snowshoe Guest Ranch with a name change in the late 1970s. They're known for exceptional mountain views, a fabulous riding program, and mouth-watering meals. According to Lisa, "We discovered this recipe and adapted it for our use in 1987 when we were looking for a tasty treat to have in the cabins for our guests. We refill the jars in the cabins each day in the summer months. I double this recipe and make it twice a week in the summer."

Makes 32 cups

- 2 sticks butter
- 1/4 cup light corn syrup
- 1/4 cup water
- 2 cups brown sugar
- 1/2 teaspoon salt
- 1 teaspoon baking soda
- 32 cups of air-popped popcorn

1. In a large saucepan, melt the butter with the corn syrup and water over medium high heat. Add the brown sugar and salt and stir until it comes to a boil. Set a timer for 5 minutes and let boil without stirring.
2. Sift the popcorn into a large bowl and be sure to remove any un-popped kernels.
3. When the timer goes off, turn off the heat and stir in the baking soda. This will cause the hot mixture to foam and almost double in size. Once incorporated, pour over the popcorn and stir well so that all pieces are covered.
4. Spread out on lined baking pans and place in a 250°F oven and bake for 20 minutes. Rotate the pans by changing shelves and switching the front to the back on each. Bake another 20 minutes.
5. Remove pans onto a cooling rack and store air tight once it has completely cooled.

★ FRANGELICO CHOCOLATE MOUSSE

Kay L Bar Ranch, Wickenburg, Arizona

Among those Civil War veterans who were owed back pay by the U.S. government at the end of the war included Thomas Valentine. Financially drained by the immense cost of the war, the government offered soldiers an opportunity to take a piece of land instead of their back pay. Valentine ventured West after the war, and in the course of his wandering, he found himself well upstream on the Sun River, at the confluence of the river's North and South Forks. There he discovered hot springs, long used by Indians for their healing properties. Wild game was abundant and land and surroundings were breathtaking.

Thomas Valentine found a piece of paradise and soon thereafter was granted, by an Act of Congress in 1872, a forty-acre tract of land as compensation for his unpaid service in the Union Army. Historically used by Indians, pioneers, trappers, and loggers, Medicine Springs (as the hot springs were known) became the province of the Klick family in 1927. Three generations of Klicks have developed the property as a guest ranch, hauling in the building materials by boat and mule train to establish guest quarters, lodge, corrals, outbuildings, and a hot springs swimming pool. Its remote location "beyond all roads," as the owners often say, the creature comforts afforded by clean and potable water, electricity to run basic lighting, refrigeration, and appliance operation are impressive.

After a day spent on Sonoran Desert trails, guests gather for family-style meals served in the historic dining room, which is one of ranch's original adobe buildings built between 1914 and 1925. Following a hearty meal, this dessert has been a guest favorite for years at the ranch and was originally created by one of our ranch chefs, Keith Larson.

Serves 6–8

3/4 cup semi-sweet chocolate, broken into pieces	1. Melt the chocolates, cocoa powder, water, and Frangelico in medium bowl set over pot of barely simmering water until smooth. Set aside to cool slightly.
1/4 cup milk chocolate, broken into pieces	
2/3 cup white chocolate chips	
4 tablespoons Dutch-processed cocoa powder	2. With an electric mixer on medium-low speed, beat egg whites in a large bowl until frothy, about 1 minute. Add cream of tartar and beat, gradually increasing speed to medium-high until whites hold soft peaks, about 2 minutes. With mixer running, slowly pour in sugar. Increase speed to high and beat until meringue becomes very thick and shiny, 2–3 minutes
3/4 cup water	
2 teaspoons Frangelico	
1 cup sugar	
6 large egg whites	
1/2 teaspoon cream of tartar	
	3. Whisk 1/3 of meringue into chocolate mixture until combined, then whisk in remaining meringue. Spoon mousse into six 6- or 8-ounce ramekins or pudding cups or large serving bowl. Cover tightly with plastic wrap. Chill overnight.

INDEX

Appetizers
- Cedar Plank Wild Mushrooms, 24
- Grilled Shrimp Cocktail, 20
- Parmesan Custard with Glazed Spring Vegetables, 26

Beef
- Meatloaf, Huckleberry Glazed, 62
- Sonoran Spice Brisket, 56
- Steak, Black Angus Rib-Eye Cowboy, 64
- Steak, Chicken Fried, 62
- Tater Tot Casserole, 59

Beverages
- Bee's Knees, 90
- Boss Man Cocktail, 58
- Cocktail, Rancho de la Osa Oquitoa, 22
- Prickly Pear Margarita, 57

Bison
- Buffaloaf, 66
- Short Ribs, 68

Bread
- Cheddar, 14
- Corn, High Altitude, 16
- Maple-Glazed Sticky Buns, 8
- Monkey, 10

Breakfast
- Bacon, Breakfast Ride Ranch Candy, 17
- Cinnamon Rolls, Tillie's, 12
- Green Chili Grits, Red Rock Ranch, 6
- Potatoes, White Stallion Ranch Ride, 5

Cakes
- Mahogany, 84
- Norwegian Cream, 86

Cookies
- Angel Thumbprint, 76
- Carrot, 75
- Cowboy, 78
- Huckleberry Lemon Crumb, 73
- Iced Oatmeal, Tim's, 74
- White Chocolate Chip, 72

Dessert
- Brownies, Maureen's Undone, 83
- Brûlée with Huckleberries, 82
- Frangelico Chocolate Mousse, 92
- Strawberry Shortcake, 88

Fish & Seafood
- Trout, Bacon & Brown Butter Cast-Iron, 46

Frosting, Icing & Toppings
- Bluberry Pie Topping, 79
- Glaze, Lemon, 73
- Icing, Almond, 74
- Icing, Orange, Sylvan Dale Ranch, 13
- Icing, Vanilla, 11

Marinades
    Chicken (Mojo Rojo), 52

Pie
    Blueberry, 79
    Rhubarb, 80

Pork
    Honey Glazed Roast, 48
    Tenderloin, Herb Crusted, 50

Poultry
    Cornish Hens, Szechuan Za'atar, 55
    Smoked Chicken Enchiladas, 60

Salad
    Broccoli, 31
    Spinach Salad w/Dressing, Ann Olson's, 30

Sauces, Toppings & Glazes
    Apple Bourbon, 51
    Bordelaise, 40
    Chipotle Salsa, 53
    Cilantro Crema, 53
    Glaze, Buffaloaf, 67
    Glaze, Honey Garlic, 42
    Glaze, Huckleberry Glaze, 63
    Gravy, white, 60
    Horseradish Black Pepper Cream, 65

Side Dishes
    Baked Beans, 34
    Mushroom Risotto, 36
    Pastina, 38
    Polenta, Jalapeno Cheddar, 37
    Quinoa, Sausage, Apple, & Pecan, 43

Snacks
    Caramel Corn, 91

Soup
    Caramelized Carrot, 23
    Chilled Corn, 28

Syrup
    Honey, 20

Vegetables
    Black Bean Puree, 52
    Carrots, Orange Bourbon, 37
    Potato Gratin, 41
    Roasted Root, 40

RANCH GLOSSARY

★ COWBOY VERNACULAR ★

Cowboys and their cooks had their own way of speaking while either on the trail or at the ranch. This is a fun throwback to those days. Author and researcher Ramon F. Adams spent years interviewing and collecting the language of the cowboy. This is a list with the main focus on food from his 1944 book, *Western Words: A Dictionary of the Range, Cow Camp and Trail.*

- **Chuck-box:** It was bolted to the rear of the chuck wagon with a hinged lid that, when let down and supported by a stout leg, forms a wide shelf or table. This is the cook's private property and woe unto the nervy puncher who tries to use it for a dining table. Occasionally this privilege is granted to the wrangler, who generally eats after all the others have finished and are changing horses, but never to a rider.
- **Cook:** Bean-master, belly cheater, biscuit roller, biscuit shooter, cocinero, cookie, cook's louse, coosie, dinero, dough-belly, dough-boxer, dough-puncher, dough roller, dough-wrangler, flunky, greasy belly, grub spoiler, grub worm, gut robber, old woman, pothooks, pot rustler, Sallie, sheffi, sop an' 'taters, sourdough, and swamper.
- **Cook Shack:** The kitchen, especially when a separate building.
- **Cook's Implements:** Dutch oven, flunky, gouch hook, lizard scorcher, pothook, round pan, squirrel can, swamper, wreck pan.
- **Coosie:** Borrowing from the Spanish, the Southwest cow country called the cook *cocinero*, and from this came the common nickname coosie.

- **Cowboy:** This word seems to have originated in Revolutionary days…The next men we find calling themselves by this name are a bunch of wild-riding, reckless Texans under the leadership of Ewen Cameron, who spent their time chasing longhorns and Mexicans soon after Texas became a republic…Then came the real cowboy as we know him today—a man who followed the cows. He has been called everything from a cow poke to a dude wrangler, but never a coward. He is still with us today and will always be as long as the West raises cows, changing, perhaps, with the times, but always witty, friendly, and fearless.
- **Cow Chips:** Dried cow or buffalo droppings. A popular fuel in the early days on the plains, where timber was scarce. It was hard to get a fire started with them, but when dry, this 'prairie coal' made a hot one.

- **Cow Grease:** A slang name for butter.
- **Crumb Castle:** A slang name for the chuck wagon.
- **Cutting the Herd:** Inspecting a trail herd for cattle which do not properly belong in it.
- **Dive/Dump:** Slang names for the bunkhouse.
- **Dough Gods:** A slang name for biscuits.
- **Dutch Oven:** A very thick, three-footed skillet with a heavy lid. It is used for cooking much of the cowboy's food, but especially biscuit. It is placed over hot coals with more coals put on the lid, thus browning the food on both sides.

- **Feed Trough:** Another slang name for the eating house.
- **Fly:** A sheet which is stretched at the end of the chuck wagon to make shade and shelter for the cook.
- **Fried Chicken:** A sarcastic name for bacon which has been rolled in flour and fried.
- **Gouch-hook:** A pot-hook used by the cook for lifting the heavy lids of his cooking utensils.
- **Greasy-sack outfit:** A small ranch outfit which carries its commissary pack in a sack on a mule in lieu of a chuck wagon.
- **Growler:** A slang name for the chuck wagon.
- **Grub house:** A slang name for the cook shack.
- **Grub-pile:** A meal; often the call to meals.
- **Gut shrunk:** Having been without food for a considerable time.
- **Hacienda:** A Spanish noun meaning a landed estate, usually the homestead of the owner, devoted to stock raising.
- **Heel squatter:** The cowboy is sometimes called thus because it is a common practice for him to rest by squatting upon his heels. This is not a comfortable seat for the layman, but the cowboy will squat comfortably on his boot-heels to eat his meals when out on the range, to spin his yarns, and, in fact, he is always ready 'to take comfort in a frog squat.'
- **Honkytonk town:** The towns at the end of the old cattle trails came under this classification, as their business districts were composed largely of saloons and honkytonks. Such towns were tough and, as the cowman would say, a 'bad place to have your gun stick.'
- **Huckydummy:** Baking powder bread with raisins.
- **Immigrant butter:** Gravy made from bacon grease, flour, and water.
- **Indian bread:** This was a tasty strip of fatty matter starting from the shoulder blade and extending backward along the backbone of a buffalo. When scalded in hot grease to seal it, then smoked, it became a tidbit the buffalo hunter used as bread. When eaten with dried meat it made an excellent sandwich.

- **Jamoka:** An occasional name for coffee made by combining Java and Mocha.
- **Jerky:** Dried beef. From the Mexican Indian word charqui (char'kee). The Spanish and the Indians first dried buffalo meat by cutting it thin and drying it in the sun. When dry, it could be ground up like meal. When cooked in a soup, it swelled to considerable proportions and served as a nourishing food. Later the white man followed their example, and jerky became a staple food.
- **John Chinaman:** What the cowboy calls boiled rice.
- **Kansas City fish:** Fried salt pork.
- **Lick:** The cowboy's name for molasses.
- **Lining his flue:** Said of one eating.
- **Lizard scorcher:** A camp stove.
- **Long sweetenin':** Slang name for molasses.

- **Machinery belting:** Tough beef.
- **Man at the pot:** If a man in camp, during meals, gets up to refill his cup with coffee and this is yelled at him, he is duty-bound by camp etiquette to go around with the pot and fill all the cups that are held out to him.
- **Mess house:** The cook shack.
- **Mess wagon:** Another name for the chuck wagon.
- **Mexican strawberries:** A slang name for dried beans.
- **Mountain oyster:** A testicle of a bull. Some find it a choice delicacy when roasted or fried.
- **Moving camp:** When a roundup camp is to be moved, the wagon boss gives instructions which no one but a cowhand familiar with the country could understand. Every cowhand finds something to do, or he is not a cowboy. Some harness the cook's teams while others help him pack and stow his pots and utensils…The mess wagon is rattling and swaying behind that running team until he wonders how the outfit holds together. By the time the cowboys reach the new camp at noon, the cook will have camp set up and a hot meal waiting for them.
- **Old woman:** Affectionate name for the cook, but said behind his back.
- **Pie-biter:** A horse which secretly forages the camp kitchen to indulge his acquired tastes.
- **Pie-box:** A slang name for the chuck wagon, perhaps in wishful thinking.
- **Pie wagon:** A trailer used behind the chuck wagon.
- **Pooch:** The name of a dish made of tomatoes, sugar, and bread.
- **Potluck:** As used by the cowman and other frontiersmen, this means food contributed by a guest. To bring potluck is to bring food with one.
- **Ram pasture:** An occasional name for the bunkhouse.
- **Sinkers:** Slang name for biscuits.

- **Skid grease:** Slang name for butter.
- **Slow elk:** To kill for food an animal belonging to someone else (as verb); beef butchered without the owner's knowledge (as noun). Some cowmen followed the philosophy that 'One's own beef don't taste as good as the other feller's because fat, tender yearling's what you kill when they're other folk's stuff.'
- **Son of a B Stew:** A favorite dish of the cowboy made of the brains, sweetbreads, and choice pieces of a freshly killed calf. If the cowhand wishes to be polite he calls it son-of-a-gun, but if no

delicate ears are present, he calls it by its true fighting name. When a calf is killed, the tongue, liver, heart, lights, kidneys, sweetbreads, and brain are carried to the cook; and he knows what is expected of him. He chops all these ingredients up into small bits with his butcher knife and prepares to stew them slowly in an iron kettle. There are as many different ways to make this dish as there are cooks. Some may throw in some potatoes, a can of tomatoes, or anything else that is handy. If the eater can tell what's in it, it is not a first-class stew. As the cowboy says, 'You throw ever'thing in the pot but the hair, horns, and holler.' The longer it is cooked the better it is.

- **Soft grub:** Hotel food, fancy victuals.
- **Sop:** Cowboy's name for gravy.
- **Sourdough bullet:** A slang name for a biscuit, not called this within hearing of the cook.
- **Sourdough keg:** A small wooden keg, usually holding about five gallons, in which the cook kept his sourdough. When getting ready for the coming roundup, the cook put three or four quarts of flour into this keg and added a dash of salt and just enough water to make a medium-thick batter. The keg was then placed in the sun to let the heat ferment the contents for several days. Sometimes a little vinegar or molasses was added to hasten the fermentation.

The first batch of batter was merely to season the keg. After the fermentation was well started, it was poured out, and enough new batter mixed up to fill the keg. Each day it was put into the sun to hasten fermentation and each night it was wrapped in blankets to keep the batter warm and working. Some cooks even slept with their kegs. After several days of this treatment, the dough was ready to use. From then to the end of the season the keg was never cleaned out. Every time the cook took out enough dough for a meal, he put back enough of the flour, salt, and water to replace it. In this way he always had plenty of dough working.

When making up his bread, he simply added enough flour and water to this batter to make a medium-stiff dough. Every wagon cook thought his sour dough the best ever, and he took great pride in his product. An outfit that let anything happen to its sourdough keg was in a bad shape, and most cooks would just about defend their kegs with their lives.

- **Sourdoughs:** Either the plural of sourdough or biscuits.
- **Sow bosom:** Salt pork.
- **Splatter dabs:** Slang name for hot cakes.
- **Spotted pup:** Rice and raisins cooked together.
- **Squirrel can:** A large can used by the cook to throw scraps into. Whenever anything, from a saddle blanket to a spur, is lost, someone jokingly suggests looking for it in the squirrel can.

- **Staked to a fill:** Given a good meal.
- **Swamp seed:** Slang name for rice.
- **Texas butter:** The cowboy's name for gravy. Put some flour into the grease in which the steak was fried and let it bubble and brown, then add hot water and stir until it thickens.
- **Whistle-berries:** The cowboy's name for beans.
- **Wreck pan:** The receptacle for the dirty dishes.

ACKNOWLEDGMENTS

A big shout out to all the ranches and their staff who kindly shared their stories and favorite recipes. Thanks to Bryce Albright, Executive Director of the Dude Ranchers Association, for putting me in touch with so many of the ranches in this book. A special thanks to Russell True, his family, and staff for sharing a wide variety of recipes from their many ranches. Also, thanks for being so hospitable and for your generosity. And last but not least, a big thanks to my publisher, Roan & Weatherford, for always believing in me.

Sherry Monahan began her writing career when she combined her passion for food, travel, and history. She penned her first book, *Taste of Tombstone,* in 1998. That same passion landed her a monthly magazine column in 2009 when she began writing her food column in *True West* entitled *Frontier Fare.* More recently, she has started another column, *Lively Libations,* discussing cocktails and spirts of the Old West in *Saddlebag Dispatches.*

Sherry is a culinary historian who enjoys researching the genealogy of food and spirits. While there's still plenty to explore about frontier food, she's expanding her culinary repertoire to include places and foods from all over America and beyond. She holds memberships in the James Beard Foundation, the Author's Guild, Single Action Shooting Society, and the Wild West History Association.

www.ingramcontent.com/pod-product-compliance
Lightning Source LLC
Chambersburg PA
CBHW060945170426
43197CB00024B/2990